READINGS ON

THE CALL OF THE WILD

Other titles in the Greenhaven Press Literary Companion Series:

AMERICAN AUTHORS

Maya Angelou
Stephen Crane
Emily Dickinson
William Faulkner
F. Scott Fitzgerald
Robert Frost
Nathaniel Hawthorne
Ernest Hemingway
Herman Melville
Arthur Miller
Eugene O'Neill
Edgar Allan Poe
John Steinbeck
Mark Twain
Walt Whitman
Thornton Wilder

AMERICAN LITERATURE

The Adventures of
  Huckleberry Finn
The Adventures of Tom
  Sawyer
The Catcher in the Rye
The Crucible
Death of a Salesman
The Glass Menagerie
The Grapes of Wrath
The Great Gatsby
Of Mice and Men
The Old Man and the Sea
The Pearl
The Scarlet Letter
A Separate Peace

BRITISH AUTHORS

Jane Austen
Joseph Conrad
Charles Dickens

BRITISH LITERATURE

Animal Farm
Beowulf
Brave New World
The Canterbury Tales
Great Expectations
Hamlet
Heart of Darkness
Julius Caesar
Lord of the Flies
Macbeth
Pride and Prejudice
Romeo and Juliet
Shakespeare: The Comedies
Shakespeare: The Histories
Shakespeare: The Sonnets
Shakespeare: The Tragedies
A Tale of Two Cities
Wuthering Heights

WORLD AUTHORS

Fyodor Dostoyevsky
Homer
Sophocles

WORLD LITERATURE

All Quiet on the Western
  Front
Antigone
The Diary of a Young Girl
A Doll's House

THE GREENHAVEN PRESS
Literary Companion
TO AMERICAN LITERATURE

READINGS ON

THE CALL OF
THE WILD

Katie de Koster, *Book Editor*

David L. Bender, *Publisher*
Bruno Leone, *Executive Editor*
Bonnie Szumski, *Series Editor*

Greenhaven Press, Inc., San Diego, CA

Every effort has been made to trace the owners of copyrighted material. The articles in this volume may have been edited for content, length, and/or reading level. The titles have been changed to enhance the editorial purpose. Those interested in locating the original source will find the complete citation on the first page of each article.

Library of Congress Cataloging-in-Publication Data

Readings on The call of the wild / Katie de Koster, book editor.
        p.   cm. — (Greenhaven Press literary companion
to American literature)
    Includes bibliographical references and index.
    ISBN 1-56510-830-2 (pbk. : alk. paper). —
ISBN 1-56510-831-0 (lib. : alk. paper)
    1. London, Jack, 1876–1916. Call of the wild.
2. Adventure stories, American—History and criticism.
3. Klondike River Valley (Yukon)—In literature.
4. Human-animal relationships in literature.
5. Wilderness areas in literature. 6. Wolves in literature.
7. Dogs in literature. I. de Koster, Katie, 1948–   .
II. Series.
PS3523.046C3836   1999
813'.512—dc21   98-48970
                                                          CIP

Cover photo: Photofest

Copyright © 1999 by Greenhaven Press, Inc.
PO Box 289009
San Diego, CA 92198-9009
Printed in the U.S.A.

66 The proper function of man is to live, not exist. I shall not waste my days in trying to prolong them. 99

Jack London

CONTENTS

Chapter 1: Klondike Adventures

Chapter 2: Themes in *The Call of the Wild*

FOREWORD

*"'Tis the good reader that
makes the good book."*

Ralph Waldo Emerson

The story's bare facts are simple: The captain, an old and scarred seafarer, walks with a peg leg made of whale ivory. He relentlessly drives his crew to hunt the world's oceans for the great white whale that crippled him. After a long search, the ship encounters the whale and a fierce battle ensues. Finally the captain drives his harpoon into the whale, but the harpoon line catches the captain about the neck and drags him to his death.

A simple story, a straightforward plot—yet, since the 1851 publication of Herman Melville's *Moby-Dick*, readers and critics have found many meanings in the struggle between Captain Ahab and the whale. To some, the novel is a cautionary tale that depicts how Ahab's obsession with revenge leads to his insanity and death. Others believe that the whale represents the unknowable secrets of the universe and that Ahab is a tragic hero who dares to challenge fate by attempting to discover this knowledge. Perhaps Melville intended Ahab as a criticism of Americans' tendency to become involved in well-intentioned but irrational causes. Or did Melville model Ahab after himself, letting his fictional character express his anger at what he perceived as a cruel and distant god?

Although literary critics disagree over the meaning of *Moby-Dick*, readers do not need to choose one particular interpretation in order to gain an understanding of Melville's novel. Instead, by examining various analyses, they can gain numerous insights into the issues that lie under the surface of the basic plot. Studying the writings of literary critics can also aid readers in making their own assessments of *Moby-Dick* and other literary works and in developing analytical thinking skills.

The Greenhaven Literary Companion Series was created with these goals in mind. Designed for young adults, this unique anthology series provides an engaging and comprehensive introduction to literary analysis and criticism. The essays included in the Literary Companion Series are chosen for their accessibility to a young adult audience and are expertly edited in consideration of both the reading and comprehension levels of this audience. In addition, each essay is introduced by a concise summation that presents the contributing writer's main themes and insights. Every anthology in the Literary Companion Series contains a varied selection of critical essays that cover a wide time span and express diverse views. Wherever possible, primary sources are represented through excerpts from authors' notebooks, letters, and journals and through contemporary criticism.

Each title in the Literary Companion Series pays careful consideration to the historical context of the particular author or literary work. In-depth biographies and detailed chronologies reveal important aspects of authors' lives and emphasize the historical events and social milieu that influenced their writings. To facilitate further research, every anthology includes primary and secondary source bibliographies of articles and/or books selected for their suitability for young adults. These engaging features make the Greenhaven Literary Companion series ideal for introducing students to literary analysis in the classroom or as a library resource for young adults researching the world's great authors and literature.

Exceptional in its focus on young adults, the Greenhaven Literary Companion Series strives to present literary criticism in a compelling and accessible format. Every title in the series is intended to spark readers' interest in leading American and world authors, to help them broaden their understanding of literature, and to encourage them to formulate their own analyses of the literary works that they read. It is the editors' hope that young adult readers will find these anthologies to be true companions in their study of literature.

INTRODUCTION: BETTER THAN THE MOVIES

The movie industry has judged *The Call of the Wild* a good story, worthy of being filmed, at least eight times. The first movie based on the tale was a sixteen-minute silent black-and-white film made in 1908 by famed director D.W. Griffith. Probably the most famous version—the first with a sound-track—was a black-and-white version made in 1935, starring Clark Gable and Loretta Young. Gable is more or less easy to identify as Thornton, but Jack London would have been surprised at his onscreen romance with Young, identified as "scrumptious" by one reviewer. Without giving away the ending, it is safe to say that with these popular romantic stars, the "tragedy" of the film is not death by Indians. Since then, other versions have featured stars as diverse as Charlton Heston, Rick Schroder, and Rutger Hauer as Thornton. The 1976 version featured a script by famed author and poet James Dickey (*Deliverance*); this one, unlike most of the others, actually focused on Buck rather than on the human actors.

The dramatic force of this short novel makes it almost irresistible to filmmakers, but they are unable to avoid one truth: Once you put the story onscreen, you lose the tremendous power of the imagination to interpret the story from Buck's point of view. Such a loss occurs any time words are translated into pictures, of course, but in *The Call of the Wild*, much of the power derives from the consistency London brings to presenting the savage wilderness through the eyes of a dog who must find his own understanding of the dangerous world into which he is thrust.

In the novel, the dog is the focus, the lens through which this world is seen, the uncomplicated interpreter of the world of man. The author's voice explains what is going on, so the reader understands, for example, why Buck is stolen, why various humans treat him differently, and what the humans are trying to achieve—all human reasons that are meaning-

11

less to Buck. But the words on the page allow the reader to slip into Buck's mind and provide a transparent interface for the imagination. London's consistency in presenting the world from Buck's point of view keeps the human element in the background. A film cannot help but disrupt that mind's-eye identification with the canine hero.

Simply put, in the book, the reader identifies with Buck, and London's words seem the thoughts and reactions of a canine, not a human. Identifying with the dog rather than with the humans gives the reader a new perspective on both the specific circumstances of the Klondike Gold Rush and more general themes of human and animal nature, greed, cruelty, kindness, and how both human and animal reactions to the harshness of nature define their spirit. This is the true accomplishment of the author, and remains one of the book's most intriguing and much-loved qualities. *Readings on* The Call of the Wild attempts to help students gain a deeper understanding of the book's themes and critical reception.

JACK LONDON: A BIOGRAPHY

As full of adventure as Jack London's books were, his life was even more adventurous. He was an oyster pirate and a seal hunter and tramped across the country as a hobo—all before he was twenty. Besides his real-life adventures, he wrote more than four dozen books, served as a war correspondent, and wrote keenly insightful reports on what he observed in his travels around the world. The amazing thing is that he packed all this living into just forty years of life.

BIRTH PARENTS AND SURROGATE PARENTS

Jack's mother, born Flora Wellman, had grown up as the youngest of five children in a prosperous family in Massillon, Ohio. When she was thirteen, an attack of typhoid affected her eyesight, made most of her hair fall out, and stunted her growth. It may also have affected the balance of her mind; from this time on, she was prone to mood swings that moved from wild enthusiasm, to black despair, to violent anger.

At the age of sixteen she drifted away from her family, heading toward the West Coast until she reached San Francisco, earning her living by a variety of methods including holding spiritualist seances and teaching music. Her spiritualism was a good match for "Professor" W.H. Chaney, a clever but irresponsible astrologer she met in San Francisco. Chaney was a charismatic vagabond in his fifties, originally from Maine, who made his living by casting horoscopes as well as writing and lecturing on many subjects. As London biographer Arthur Calder-Marshall describes Chaney,

> Like so many self-educated men of his time, he was sure that he had the answers to all the important questions of his day. He was a pioneer socialist. He wrote about "The Causes and Cure of Poverty" and "What's to Be Done with the Criminal?" He was as convinced that God did not exist as he was that he could foretell the future by the position of the stars at the moment of anyone's birth.

The unconventional pair lived together as man and wife without bothering to get married. As Chaney later wrote to Jack London, "A very loose condition of society was fashionable at San Francisco at the time. . . . It was not thought disgraceful for two to live together without marriage." The arrangement seemed to suit them both until Flora Wellman became pregnant at the age of thirty-three. Then, according to Wellman—who was calling herself Mrs. Chaney—the Professor insisted she get an abortion or he would leave. She refused, and made two ineffective attempts at suicide, trying first to overdose on laudanum (a product of opium), then shooting herself in the forehead with a revolver, resulting in a flesh wound.

The newspapers of the day delighted in such dramatic stories. The *San Francisco Chronicle* headlined the story "Driven from Home for Refusing to Destroy Her Unborn Infant—A Chapter of Heartlessness and Domestic Misery," while the *San Francisco Bulletin* reported that "the unfortunate woman is the wife of a notorious charlatan and missionary of the Woodhull School who styles himself Professor Chaney, and her despair was caused by the desertion and brutal treatment of this fellow." With sympathy firmly against him, Chaney denied his paternity—suggesting several other possible fathers among the couple's circle—and fled to Oregon. He never communicated with Wellman again. Jack did not learn the circumstances of his birth for many years; when he did, he wrote to Chaney, who said Jack was not his son.

Opinion is divided as to whether Chaney was in fact Jack London's father. London biographer Robert Barltrop writes,

> Jack's father, William Chaney, was an exceptional man. Both Irving Stone [who wrote a biographical novel about London] and Joan London [Jack's elder daughter] believed there was a striking physical resemblance between him and Jack. Chaney was short, sturdily built and vigorous. The doctor who attended Flora during her pregnancy is said to have recognised Jack London, at sixteen, as Chaney's son. To attribute adventurousness, intellectual power and financial irresponsibility to the relationship depends on one's view of heredity; nevertheless, both men had them.

On the other hand, Clarice Stasz, author of *American Dreamers,* a biography of Jack and Charmian London (Jack's second wife), gives some credence to William Chaney's denials of paternity:

> Many have accepted Chaney as Jack's biological father; Jack's daughter Joan worked on a biography to redeem the reputa-

tion of the man she believed to be her grandfather. Yet the circumstantial evidence speaks against this possibility as much as for it. There is neither a striking resemblance nor lack of one in the two men's faces. Although Chaney had been a ladies' man who had had six legal wives, he had failed to impregnate any woman before or after Flora.

There were no DNA tests in 1876 to determine who was the father of Flora Wellman's child. Whoever he was, he played no role in Jack's life after the child was born. And, as Stasz points out, "It is less important to know who Jack's real father was than to know that Flora was left to carry and bear the child without a mate."

The baby, first named John Chaney and called Johnnie, was born January 12, 1876. Flora Wellman was too weak to nurse the infant, and he was sent to live with a wet nurse, Virginia Daphne Prentiss, called Mammy Jenny. Jenny, an ex-slave, was married to a white carpenter; they had recently lost a baby in childbirth. She adored the baby, who stayed with her for eight months. Jenny later recalled that Flora

> was on the go from morning till night. . . . She seemed to be sad and angry at the same time, and all the time, but her angriness would not let her just be sad for a while and get over it, but kept driving her and driving her. I took care of her baby, but she was so busy that she couldn't even come to see him very often.

The bond established between Mammy Jenny and Jack would remain close all his life. Unfortunately, the warmth of Jenny's affection was in stark contrast to his birth mother's attitude. Perhaps because her pregnancy caused the breakup of her relationship with Chaney, Jack's mother never had a loving bond with her child. In her book *Jack London: An American Radical?* Carolyn Johnston wrote, "Although Flora chose to have the child, she seemed to resent motherhood. . . . Flora seldom laughed, was undemonstrative, and inflicted severe psychological wounds on her son almost from the moment of his birth. The child desperately wanted to be loved and accepted, so he turned more to his black surrogate mother than to his own."

Stasz admits that "Flora has often been blamed for Jack's sense of desperate loss, and it is hard to exonerate her. He was her only natural child, yet she would not show him affection or provide reassurance. It was their common tragedy that he perceived her influence as totally negative." Yet she goes on to note that Jack "may also have blocked signs of Flora's caring. Certainly she made every effort to provide for the family's physical needs." And perhaps Flora, the materially indulged youngest child of a wealthy family, simply had little knowledge of how to provide maternal affection; her own mother had died shortly after she was born.

Flora Wellman met an Iowa widower, John London, in San Francisco, probably in early 1876. London had seven living children (four had died), although only his youngest daughters, Eliza and Ida, lived with him in California. Flora and John were married on September 7, 1876. The eight-month-old John Chaney was renamed John Griffith London (he chose the nickname Jack for himself a few years later), and Flora's new husband accepted her son as his own. Although a couple of his sons visited their father and stepmother once or twice in later years, London's other children remained in Iowa, being cared for by relatives.

Although Mammy Jenny remained an important caregiver in Jack's life, the newlywed couple brought Jack home to live with them and John's daughters Eliza and Ida. Eliza London, just six years older than Jack, became his new surrogate mother. By the time he was four years old, Jack was going to school with Eliza. Robert Barltrop reports,

> The mothering of little Jack was done largely by his sister Eliza. In San Francisco she wheeled him in his perambulator, at Alameda she took him to school with her. The teacher gave him a box for his desk and picture-books to look at; this is probably the explanation for his being able to say later that he could read and write at the age of five without recollecting being taught to do either.

John London also showed his stepson affection; Jack later said of him that he was "kind, always kind." He took Jack out sailing, teaching him skills that would later serve him in his adventures around the world. "My father was the best man I have ever known," Jack said of him, "too intrinsically good to get ahead in the soulless scramble for a living that a man must cope with if he would survive in our anarchical capitalist system."

AN UNSETTLED CHILDHOOD

While Jack's surrogate parents—Mammy Jenny, stepsister Eliza, and stepfather John London—all treated him with the affection he did not receive from his birth parents, the Londons' family life was both difficult and unsettled. The family moved often, sometimes half a dozen times in one year. Having grown up in luxury, Flora was determined to live that way again. She pushed her husband into a variety of business decisions that seemed wise or at least workable at the time, but all led to failure, often from overreaching.

Moving his family to Oakland, across the bay from San Francisco, John London bought some land and began raising vegetables to sell in a small shop. He returned from a trip to find that his partner had robbed him, taking off with all their money, and he had to start over again, moving to Alameda, then to San Mateo along the coast, and then to a small ranch in the Livermore Valley. Each time his hard work began to pay off, Flora would urge him to expand his holdings by mortgaging what he held and buying more land, vines, orchards, chickens, horses. At the same time, she tried to instill in her son the idea that they were better than their neighbors. As Carolyn Johnston puts it,

> Her values were of the upper, genteel class. She taught her son the precepts of Anglo-Saxon superiority and emphasized that they were the only "Americans" in the vicinity—clearly denigrating their Irish and Italian neighbors. . . . Always she longed for the pride and security of her genteel childhood. Flora's insistence that they were better than their neighbors and that, while poor, they were respectable made her son feel ashamed of his condition and determined to rise out of his class.

The children were expected to pitch in to help with the family enterprises, while Flora turned her hand to a variety of moneymaking plans, from holding seances (she terrified Jack when her "Indian control, Plume" began screaming war chants through his mother's voice) to starting a kindergarten and selling lottery tickets. Eliza, made responsible for the chicken-and-egg business at the ranch in Livermore, finally grew tired of the drudgery and eloped with an older man at the age of sixteen or seventeen. The ranch failed, the bank foreclosed, and the family moved back to Oakland, where Flora attempted to run a boardinghouse. This too failed, and John, who had lost a lung during the Civil War, finally gave up entrepreneurship. Over the next few years he took a series of jobs, usually as a constable or night watchman.

Mammy Jenny had moved to Oakland to be close to Jack, and Eliza and her husband settled nearby. But of almost equal importance to Jack was that he now lived near a public library. Since a person could only check out a certain number of books at a time, Jack had Eliza's family apply for tickets he could use as well as his own. The librarian, Ina Coolbrith, noticed the eleven-year-old voracious reader and took him under her wing. Robert Barltrop writes that Miss Coolbrith was his first contact with a cultured person, and Jack was fascinated as well as grateful. Finding that his greatest enjoyment was books of travel, adventure, and discovery, she supplied everything she could. He read obsessively, continually exciting his emotions.

Among Jack's favorite books were those that told of fame and riches awaiting those who worked hard; he especially loved Ouida's novel *Signa,* which told the tale of the illegitimate child of an artist and a peasant girl, who escaped the drudgery of Italian village life and won great fame by his skill in playing and composing music. As he recalled later, "Reading the story, my narrow hill-horizon was pushed back, and all the world made possible if I would dare it. I dared."

WORK, WORK, WORK

Jack was getting up before dawn to deliver newspapers, then delivering more papers after school each day, earning about twelve dollars a month (of which Flora allowed him to keep ten cents a week for himself). When he was about twenty, ten years later, he wrote to a friend about this period of his life:

> Duty!—at ten years I was on the street selling newspapers....
> I had no childhood. Up at three o'clock in the morning to carry papers. When that was finished I did not go home but continued on to school. School out, my evening papers. Saturday I worked on an ice wagon; Sunday I went to a bowling alley and set up pins for drunken Dutchmen.

Jack didn't tell Flora about all the money he earned, though. He hung around the Yacht Club on the estuary, scrubbing decks and doing other odd jobs for a few cents, and learning his way around boats. He saved his pennies and, when he was thirteen, he had two dollars—enough to buy an old, leaky boat. He sailed it up and down the estuary and even out into the bay, learning to handle it by trial and error, applying lessons learned from John London in earlier years about wind, currents, and tides. London biographer Andrew Sinclair describes his adventures on the "bright treacherous seas" of San Francisco Bay:

> His happiest hours as a child had been with John London, rowing and fishing in the vast sea-shell of waters pent within the inlet through the Golden Gate. Now he taught himself to sail dangerously on the choppy and foggy waters, crashing the rollers made by the sidewheel steamers, beating against the wind to Goat Island, yearning at the clippers that tacked toward the west and the other side of the world.

It wouldn't be long before he was following those yearnings. In the meantime, John London was out of work and had suffered serious injuries, reportedly from being struck by a train. Jack left school after finishing the eighth grade and took a job at a local cannery, working long hours for little money—most of which he turned over to his mother. It wasn't long before he concocted a scheme for making much more money with less effort: he would become an oyster pirate.

The most productive oyster beds in the area were controlled by monopolies, such as the Southern Pacific Railroad. Raiding the beds was a popular pastime for those who would be called juvenile delinquents today, although they were helped by widespread public sympathy for their thievery. Jack borrowed three hundred dollars from Jenny to buy a boat, the *Razzle Dazzle* and began his short career as what he described as "the Prince of the Oyster Pirates" at the age of sixteen. He later wrote about this time in *The Cruise of the Dazzler*.

JOURNEY TO MANHOOD

Being an oyster pirate—even a hard-working, drinks-buying one—had other drawbacks than the obvious one of being illegal. There was a fair amount of rivalry among the young men, and competitors finally burned his boat. He briefly teamed up with another pirate, then accepted an offer from the California Fish Patrol to put in his efforts on the right side of the law: he began helping apprehend the men who had briefly been his comrades. The job had no salary, but he was allowed to keep half the fines levied on the pirates he caught—a formidable motivation for using his best efforts to pursue his old friends. A few years later, he would enhance and serialize these adventures for *Youth's Companion* magazine in stories that were finally collected as *Tales of the Fish Patrol*.

During this period, while John London was working at low-paying jobs, Jack was able to help support his family more reliably and in more comfort than they had known for years. Yet tensions were growing at home; his mother complained that he was "bossy." His stepsister Ida had married and had a child, Johnny Miller. Ida often left young Johnny with Flora, who, according to Andrew Sinclair, "lavished on Johnny all the love she had withheld from Jack. Jealous and bitter, her own son stayed on the waterfront, struggling and surviving through his fists and cunning."

After one night of drunken carousing, Jack fell into the water and was swept out to sea. He decided it was a good way to die and didn't try to swim to shore for several hours. By the time he sobered up and realized he wanted to live, it was almost too late; he was saved by a Greek fisherman who happened to spot him in the water.

Realizing the Fish Patrol had little future for him, he decided to ride the rails with some young hobos known as "road kids." They called him "Sailor Kid" and accepted him into their freewheeling lifestyle for a few weeks; then he moved on again, restless for he knew not what. He wandered back to the waterfront and, finding a sealing fleet wintering in the bay, got to know some of the crews. Within a few days of his seventeenth birthday, he signed on as an able-bodied seaman on a three-masted schooner called the *Sophie Sutherland.* The boat sailed with no liquor on board, and wages were to be paid only at the end of a seven-month voyage.

The *Sophie Sutherland* sailed for Hawaii, then north to hunt seals in the waters off Japan and Siberia, weathering a typhoon in the waters near Japan. The seal butchery was bloody work; as he described it in *The Sea-Wolf* a few years later,

> After a good day's killing I have seen our decks covered with hides and bodies, slippery with fat and blood, the scuppers running red; masts, ropes, and rails spattered with the sanguinary color; and the men, like butchers plying their trade, naked and red of arm and hand, hard at work with ripping and flensing knives, removing the skins from the pretty sea creatures they had killed.

This venture, as Andrew Sinclair notes, "was the young sailor's first sight of nature red in tooth and claw. The men were more bestial than the beasts they killed. . . . Jack began to see that the struggle to live among humans was part of the struggle to live among animals"—sentiments that would find expression in many of his later works, including *The Call of the Wild.*

The hard work and camaraderie on the boat proved invigorating and helped clear Jack of the demoralization he had been feeling. He had taken a pile of books with him, reading every chance he got, and on his return he was determined to find a steady job and spend his spare time studying, rather than drinking, so he could improve his life.

Finding a job wasn't so easy though; financial panic hit the country in 1893, and thousands were out of work. He took a job in a jute mill working at a burlap machine for ten cents an hour—the same wage he had earned at the cannery when he left school at thirteen.

The one bright spot in his life right then was a writing competition run by the *San Francisco Morning Call* for amateur writers. He wrote a two-thousand-word tale, "Story of a Typhoon off the Coast of Japan," based on his seal-hunting voyage, and was tremendously excited when he won first prize. The twenty-five-dollar award was as much as he earned in a month, but even more important was the idea that he might break free of the physical grind of manual labor and write to earn money. He quickly sent in more stories to the newspaper, but the quality required for professional writing was much higher than that needed to win an amateur contest. He submitted stories to a few other markets, which also rejected them. His hopes were dashed almost as quickly as they had soared.

When he didn't receive a promised raise at the jute mill to $1.25 a day, he switched jobs and shoveled coal for the Oakland street railway's power station, earning $30 a month until he learned that he had replaced two men who had each been earning $40 a month. He quit in anger, both at the thought of having cost two men their jobs and at having been pushed to work so hard. He began to wonder if he was to be a "work beast" his entire life.

ON THE ROAD

As unemployment levels in the country rose, laborers looking for work joined the hobos in riding the rails—hopping on freight trains to travel across country. The unemployed began to band together, calling themselves an "army" and their leaders "generals." "General" Jacob S. Coxey organized a national march on Washington, "Coxey's Army," to demand help from the government. In the Oakland area, an activist named Charles Kelly rallied men to join the march. London decided to join "Kelly's Army," one of many groups that joined Coxey's movement.

The group was to set out from Oakland on April 6, 1894, and Jack showed up at the appointed time with ten dollars he'd borrowed from Eliza. But the local government was uneasy about the massing of so many unhappy men, and the army heard a rumor that their leader, Kelly, was to be arrested. The group had departed hurriedly during the night before London arrived, so he set out a few hours after the main group had boarded the trains, catching up with them in Council Bluffs, Iowa.

Kelly's group was on foot now, in rain and bitter cold weather, although many people in the communities they passed through were sympathetic to their goal, and often provided food for them. London stayed with the group, walking toward Des Moines during the day, discussing economics and politics around campfires at night. Robert Barltrop writes,

> This was where Jack London first heard socialism being expounded and discussed. Like all demonstrations of its sort, the army of the unemployed was made up principally of working men in whom radical consciousness had already been roused. A high proportion were trade unionists. . . . From their talk of books and theories of society Jack was given a new perspective on his experiences in the cannery and the power-station. Listening, he saw the position of the working class as a trap from which he had to escape.

From Des Moines, the group decided to make rafts that would take them by river along their route toward Washington, scouting for supplies along the way. With Jack's boating skills, he quickly became one of the leading rafters; he and his crew would get ahead of the other crews and take for themselves the cream of the food and supplies offered by the farmers and communities along the river. As Robert Barltrop puts it,

> His experience and skill quickly put him and his nine-man crew ahead of all the rest, and his proficiency at begging and scrounging brought them the best of the countrysides' pickings. In a short time the other crews were angry. . . . While [Jack's crew] lived well on food, coffee and tobacco, the army following behind went hungry.

Kelly eventually sent horsemen around to tell the area residents that his army disowned the efforts of these "pirates" who claimed to represent the entire group but served mainly themselves. Thereafter Jack and his crew were forced to remain with the main contingent instead of being allowed to travel ahead of it, a punishment Jack resented; he saw his endeavors as a bit of a lark, a use of initiative and ability that should have been rewarded. As Barltrop concludes, such an attitude "leaves out that it took place at everyone else's expense. The doctrine of the survival of the fittest, which was to be a dominant theme in Jack's stories, was already affirmed in his outlook. Loyalty, which he extolled . . . as the greatest of virtues, was always over-ridden by his conviction that he would be top dog and the weaker others would go to the wall."

The army was falling apart, and Jack joined several of his fellows in deserting the group on May 24, at Hannibal, Missouri. For the next year he traveled around the country, once again using his scrounging skills to his own benefit, visiting relatives, hopping freight trains, sightseeing in Canada, New York, Boston, Baltimore, frequently making notes in his diary about what he observed on the road.

At the end of June 1894 he was in New York to see Niagara Falls and for the first time suffered an experience that was a common occurrence for most of his fellow tramps: he was arrested for vagrancy. Shackled to more than a dozen other men in court the next morning, he watched as each man was pronounced guilty and sentenced to thirty days without making a plea or presenting evidence. When it was his turn, he decided, he would insist on his right to a trial; this was America, after all. His name was called, he started to speak, the judge told him to shut up, and he was sentenced to thirty days in the penitentiary with the rest of the men. He was stunned to find that vagrants were granted none of the rights the justice system was supposed to provide to all citizens.

Conditions were harsh in jail, and weaker prisoners were prey to both guards and other prisoners. Jack survived by befriending an older prisoner who knew the ropes, but the brutality of his month-long experience in jail and his sense of moral outrage at the way he and others were treated were powerfully described years later in his book *The Road.*

BACK TO SCHOOL

Jack now had two firm resolves: to escape from the drudgery of low-paying jobs of physical labor, and to stay out of jail. He continued his tramp travels for a while longer, but eventually made his way back to his family in Oakland, determined to go to high school. Although he was three or four years older than his classmates and impatient, he managed to stay in school for one year, during which he contributed several stories and articles to the school newspaper. By the spring of 1896, though, he decided to leave school and cram for the university entrance exams for the University of California. He did well enough in the midsummer tests to be admitted to the fall class as a probationary student at the age of twenty. Reports London biographer Franklin Walker, "London was in college with serious intent and wasted not a moment on the customary undergraduate foolishness. His reputation as a socialist who had been a sailor and a hobo encouraged him in a role which emphasized maturity." He managed to make it through one semester, then dropped out.

The reason for his dropping out has been debated among London's biographers. He was impatient; he was poor and could not afford the fees; he found the teachers shallow and opposed to new ideas. Barltrop believes he dropped out because this was when he discovered that John London was not his father and that he was illegitimate: "The consequences were bound to be catastrophic. Illegitimacy was a huge personal and social stain, a reason in itself why one could not continue at university." Whatever the reason, he requested and was granted an honorable dismissal from the university in February 1897.

The New Goal: Becoming a Writer

London decided to run for the Oakland Board of Education on the Socialist-Labor ticket during the spring elections that year, an enterprise with no hope of success but a certain amount of fun—and public recognition: the *Oakland Times* mentioned that he "is recognized among a certain set as a leader in socialism, and is thought to be a bright fellow." While this did not get him elected, he may have thought getting his name before the public could only help in his real ambition: to become a writer.

He wasn't yet producing publishable material, so he took a job in a laundry at a military academy, intending to write during his spare time. The job was so exhausting, though, that for the first time in years he didn't even have the energy to read, much less to write. When the academy closed for the summer, he was casting about for another job when he heard the news brought in by a few unkempt men on the S.S. *Excelsior.*

The Klondike

The *Excelsior* docked in San Francisco on July 14, 1897. The announcement that it carried several men who had struck it rich by finding gold in the area around the Klondike River in Canada electrified thousands of those who, like Jack, were looking for both adventure and a way to make their fortune. Gold fever also struck his sister Eliza's elderly husband, Captain James Shepard. The Shepards mortgaged their home to put together a grubstake, and Shepard offered to take Jack along as his partner; Jack's contribution would be physical rather than financial. On July 25, just eleven days after the

Excelsior had delivered its electrifying news, Shepard and London embarked on the S.S. *Umatilla* carrying a year's worth of supplies—about a ton apiece.

Shepard regretted the rashness of his decision soon after they landed in Juneau, Alaska, when he faced one of the first obstacles on the trail to the Klondike, the Chilkoot Pass. They had been told to expect to pay Indian porters six cents a pound to transport their two tons of supplies across the pass, but by the time they arrived, the price had risen to thirty cents a pound, and went to fifty cents while they were trying to decide what to do. The Canadians insisted that everyone crossing the border into Canada, to reach the Klondike, had to have five hundred dollars in cash and a thousand pounds of food; the customs house, at the Canadian border, was near the summit of the pass. London and Shepard realized that if they paid the porters, they wouldn't have enough money; if they abandoned part of their supplies, they'd be sent back for having insufficient food. The only option was to carry the supplies over the pass themselves.

Shepard had suffered a mild heart attack just before they left San Francisco, and knew he wasn't up to this effort. He returned home on the boat that had brought them to Alaska, leaving Jack with their combined supplies and his share of the money. Jack continued with three men he had met on the boat; the four of them had 5,000 pounds of supplies to carry up a steep, slushy path that had been stirred up by the feet of hundreds of heavily laden men. Each man carried 150 pounds at a time, making four trips a day. Just getting all their supplies to the head of the pass took two and a half days—and there were twenty-two miles of porterage between them and Lake Lindeman, where they could switch to boats for passage downstream.

The trail to the lake was an obstacle course that had to be covered several times, as they carried and cached one load of supplies and went back for more, over and over again. But once they reached the lake, Jack's talents helped them pull ahead of many of the pack of men who were fighting for places on boats. He and his partners built their own craft, named the *Yukon Belle;* Jack sewed the sails.

The boat carried them to Lake Marsh, where two areas of rapids in the water had halted many of the prospective prospectors. Some had tried to shoot the rapids and had failed, losing their gear or even their lives. Others were trying a difficult portage around the rapids, while most were simply stumped, unsure what to do.

Jack walked down to scout out the rapids, then told his partners that the *Yukon Belle* would be able to get through safely. They trusted him with their lives and, when the boat made it in just a couple of minutes, many of the people stranded begged him to take them through, too. He returned to fulfill a promise to one man and his wife, because he felt it gallant that a woman should accompany her husband in such a venture, then he and his partners continued. It was, after all, a race, with the prospect of staking a lucrative claim the goal.

By October 9 the four men had reached an encampment of abandoned fur traders' huts on the Upper Island on the Henderson River. They decided to spend the winter there, along with many of their fellow prospectors, and set out to pan some of the side streams in the area. On the twelfth they found an area of sand full of gleaming grains, and they quickly staked out their claim and started calculating the expected yield.

They had to register the claims they had staked in order to claim them, so they kept quiet while they surveyed the whole area, made a map of the area they wanted to claim, and gathered a bag of the shiny dust. After four days, they rushed to Dawson City to register their claim—only to be laughed at by the assayer, who told them their rich strike was mica, not gold.

After pushing so hard for so long, and getting so excited about their claim, the news was a severe letdown. The men decided to stay in town until their money ran out, hanging out in the saloons and gathering tales from all the people they met there.

This prospecting for the stories that were to become London's "gold" continued after the men returned to Upper Island, where about seventy men were prepared to spend the long winter months. One of those, a man named Hargrave, was fascinated by Jack, whom he called a genius. He later recalled Jack's intense intellectual curiosity, as he questioned everyone he met, including native Alaskans:

> Everything interested him, events, things, men—all kinds and manner of men. To the others a native was a "siwash," but Jack would talk to them, in so far as his limited command of Chinook and their even more restricted command of English would permit. He would entertain them and invite them into the cabin, and I believe that he learned more about them, their customs, their primitive souls, than was known to the oldest sourdough squaw on the river.

It wasn't hardship or the failure to find gold that made London leave the Klondike, but scurvy. This disabling ailment, now known to be caused by lack of vitamin C, struck the men who lived on biscuit, beans, and bacon, and had no fresh fruit or vegetables. When the spring thaw came, he and his cabin mate dismantled their cabin and used its logs to make a raft. They floated it down to Dawson, where they sold the logs to a lumbermill for several hundred dollars. Taken to the hospital, London was told his only hope for survival was to return to a place where he could find fresh food. As he began his return trip to California, he recorded these few words about his health:

> Given some fresh potatoes and a can of tomatoes for my scurvy, which has now almost crippled me from my waist down. Right leg drawing up; can no longer straighten it; even in walking must put my whole weight on toes. These few raw potatoes and tomatoes are worth more to me at the present stage of the game than an Eldorado claim.

London returned to Oakland with only $4.50 worth of gold dust, but with a treasure lode of experiences that would eventually help him strike it rich as a writer.

A NEW CAREER

On his return to California Jack learned that John London had died; his mother, who was trying to raise Ida's son Johnny in a tiny cottage, was in debt and struggling to pay off creditors. He registered at several employment agencies, took Civil Service exams for postman, and turned his hand to whatever small casual jobs he could find, but work was hard to come by. When he wasn't working or looking for work, he was writing and submitting manuscripts to newspapers and magazines. The works were based on his recent adventures, but he had not yet learned to craft the story and give it a dramatic theme, and all were rejected. He pawned his belongings and continued to write, while the grocer stopped his credit (he owed four dollars) and the butcher did the same (after five dollars in unpaid bills).

The acceptance that started the ball rolling was from the *Overland Monthly*, a well-respected magazine founded by Bret Harte, which unfortunately was almost as broke as he was. The editors were slow to pay, but they were so sympathetic to London's work that he kept sending them manuscripts. They hoped this new writer would bring them new readers, and he knew exposure in the magazine would bring him legitimacy in the eyes of better-paying markets. His first story, "To the Man on the Trail," appeared in the January 1889 issue of the magazine, for which they eventually paid

$5.00. The following month, *Black Cat* magazine paid him $40.00 for a horror story, "A Thousand Deaths," while the *Overland Monthly* offered him a contract for six more stories at $7.50 each, with the promise of a prominent position in the magazine to make up for the small payment.

At this stage of his life, poised on the brink of a successful and prolific writing career, the "boy author" (as the Oakland newspapers were calling him) described himself for a correspondent:

> 23 years of age last January. Stand five feet seven or eight in stocking feet—sailor life shortened me. At present time weigh 168 lbs; but readily jump same pretty close to 180 when I take up outdoor life and go to roughing it. Am clean shaven—when I let 'em come, blonde moustache and black whiskers—but they don't come long. Clean face makes my age enigmatical, and equally competent judges variously estimate my age from twenty to thirty. Greenish-grey eyes, heavy brows which meet; brown hair. . . . Face bronzed through many long-continued liaisons with the sun, though just now, owing to bleaching process of sedentary life, it is positively yellow. Several scars—hiatus of eight front upper teeth, usually disguised with false plate. There I am in toto.

SUCCESS

Soon London was selling shorter pieces regularly to a variety of magazines and papers, stories of all sorts and essays on socialism. By July 1899—just one year after he had returned from the Klondike—London had sold a long short story to the prestigious *Atlantic Monthly* for $120.00. With this coup, he collected several of his published stories and submitted them to Houghton Mifflin, who published them as *The Son of the Wolf* in the spring of 1900. Robert Barltrop quotes the publisher's reader's report, recommending acceptance of the manuscript, to show why he was rapidly becoming popular:

> He uses the current slang of the mining camps a little too freely, but his style has freshness, vigor and strength. He draws a vivid picture of the terrors of the cold, darkness and starvation, the pleasures of human companionship in adverse circumstances, and the sterling qualities which the rough battle with nature brings out. The reader is convinced that the author has lived the life himself.

By the end of 1899, flyers announcing his lecture to the Socialist Labor Party were dubbing him "The Distinguished Magazine Writer." Within the next few months, he and his mother were able to move into a larger house, and on the day his first book was published, April 7, 1900, he married Bess Maddern.

A SUDDEN MARRIAGE

London seems to have decided to marry on the spur of the moment, perhaps because he finally felt he was in a position to be able to support a family. He treated his decision as a business deal, certainly not a romance; as he wrote to a friend, "Sunday morning, last, I had not the slightest intention of doing what I am going to do. I came down and looked over the house I was to move into—that fathered the thought. I made up my mind. Sunday evening I opened transactions for a wife; by Monday evening had the affair well under way; and next Saturday morning I shall marry. . . . I shall be steadied, and can be able to devote more time to my work."

Love does not seem to have been a dominant emotion in the transaction. Bess, who had tutored Jack in mathematics the summer he was studying for the entrance examinations to the university, had been engaged to a man who had died. Jack, who saw the new house as a place where his friends could gather, wanted a hostess for his home and a mother to bear his children—he hoped for "seven Saxon sons." In fact, Jack seems to have been in love with Anna Strunsky, described by Barltrop as "a seventeen-year-old Russian Jewess of great beauty and rich intellect"; some have surmised that Anna had refused to marry him, while others suggest Jack was looking for a quiescent spouse who would not be tempestuous and intellectually stimulating, as Anna was. Jack and Anna would later write *The Kempton-Wace Letters,* in which they debated the nature of love, and a few years later Bess would mistakenly name Anna as co-respondent in her divorce suit against Jack.

At first, though, the newlyweds seemed happy enough together. Jack found a cottage nearby for Flora and Johnny Miller, so the couple had the new house to themselves but could also entertain a new circle of friends, the young bohemians of San Francisco, who called themselves the Crowd, according to Andrew Sinclair. Besides Anna Strunsky, his new friends included George Sterling, a young poet who was a protégé of Ambrose Bierce. Sterling exposed London to a life of breeding and taste, while London introduced his new friend to a world of rough pleasure and physical and intellectual vigor. London called Sterling "Greek," and Sterling called London "Wolf," a reference both to the heroes (man and beast) of the tales he was writing and to his position as "lone wolf" even in a crowd. Another of his new friends was

Charmian Kittredge, an emancipated woman of about thirty who enjoyed dueling with Jack with a fencing foil or boxing gloves.

As success brought a level of financial security Jack had never known, he was determined to enjoy the childhood he felt he had missed. He and Bess moved to better and better homes, and he loved to entertain and drink with his friends. Bess was less comfortable with the Crowd, and after the births of their daughters, Joan in 1901 and Becky in 1902, she withdrew, disapproving of their boisterous and unconventional lifestyle.

A SOCIALIST SPOKESMAN

In 1902, London spent a few weeks in the East End slums of London, appalled at the poverty and misery he found there, which he recorded in *People of the Abyss.* (He had agreed to an assignment covering the Boer War, but it ended before he arrived; not wanting to return home to a failing marriage, he went instead to London.) The sympathy he expressed in this book helped him gain credence as a proletarian author. He had long espoused a socialist philosophy, seeming unaware of the disparity between his professed views, his survival-of-the-Anglo-Saxon-fittest philosophy, and his enjoyment of the fruits of a capitalist system of rewards.

The Call of the Wild was published to great acclaim in 1903. In 1904, broke and separated from his wife (he spent money as quickly as it came in, and Bess had had her lawyer place attachments on all of his property, including literary works), London accepted an assignment covering the war between Japan and Russia; the fame he gained by his fine journalism as well as tales of his aggressiveness in going after stories helped put his next book, *The Sea-Wolf,* at the top of the best-seller list in 1904. By the time his essay collection *The War of the Classes* was published in 1905, Jack had become a valuable spokesman for leftist causes. He was elected the first president of the Intercollegiate Socialist Society, a post that all agreed was a figurehead. Upton Sinclair, founder of the society (and an author who would become famous for his book *The Jungle* three years later), helped arrange a wildly successful national lecture tour for London. Of course, not everyone supported socialism, and apparently some of those who objected were willing to use personal attacks on the speaker to prevent him from appearing. They caused the only disturbances during the tour, convincing a few places to cancel his appearances in protest because he had married Charmian Kittredge on November 19, the day after his divorce from Bessie became final, in apparent violation of a state law that decreed a waiting period of one year.

It was also as a Socialist that Jack ran for the office of mayor of Oakland. Like his earlier foray into politics, he never expected to win, but considered it important that the party make a showing in the election.

THE *SNARK* AND BEAUTY RANCH

A few months before his marriage to Charmian, Jack had started acquiring land near Glen Ellen in California. The first purchase was a small ranch of nearly 130 acres, thickly wooded with redwoods, manzanita, and live oak trees. This would be the starting point for what would become Beauty Ranch, the site of Wolf House, planned as "the ancestral home of the first of the great London dynasty," as London biographer Arthur Calder-Marshall reports. Over the years he added to the parcel of land, usually going into debt he could ill afford to buy each new plot.

Another project absorbing his rapidly rising income was the building of a boat, the *Snark*, on which he and Charmian planned to take a seven-year around-the-world voyage. When the great San Francisco earthquake of 1906 destroyed much of the city (Jack reported on the aftermath of the quake for *Collier's*), building supplies became scarce; Jack paid black-market prices for the material to complete the building of his boat. It was finally launched on April 23, 1907, but was hardly "the tightest ship afloat" Jack had declared it to be. As Clarice Stasz reports,

> The *Snark* was a sieve. The sides leaked, the bottom leaked, the self-bailing cockpit flooded. The gasoline in supposedly nonleakable tanks behind a supposedly airtight bulkhead filtered out to contaminate the foodstuffs and turn the craft into a floating bomb. The dynamo refused to deliver power to the lights. In the bathroom, Jack's special pride, the pipes burst the first day out, ruining all hopes of modern hygiene.

It didn't handle well, and the crew Jack had assembled was generally either incompetent or uninterested in the hard work required to keep the boat afloat and in good shape. Nonetheless, despite newspaper reports that the boat was presumed lost and its passengers drowned, they made it to Hawaii, entering the port of Honolulu on May 21, where they were welcomed as celebrities by the islands' social and business leaders. Both Jack and Charmian wrote stories and articles about their five-month stay in Hawaii. On October 7, the repaired and repainted *Snark* set sail again, heading out of the port of Hilo toward the Marquesas Islands, eight hundred miles northeast of Tahiti—a passage considered impossible because of the unfavorable wind conditions. This Jack took as a challenge—a challenge he met, for after a perilous journey, they reached the Marquesas in early December.

Landing in Tahiti in January, the Londons found three months' worth of accumulated mail, including correspondence indicating that they were nearly broke. They took a steamship to San Francisco in January, staying in Oakland for a week to straighten out their finances, then returned the same way to Tahiti, remaining there for a couple of months so Jack could concentrate on his writing. After he finished *Martin Eden* and sent it off to his publisher, they were off again, this time to the Society Islands; from there, it was on to American Samoa, and then to the Fiji Islands. When they arrived in the New Hebrides, the local missionary assured them no white man had been killed there for thirty years, although the natives were still eating each other just five miles inland. In the Solomon Islands, "where white heads hanging behind a chieftain's chair were of highest value as a display of strength," according to Clarice Stasz, they kept all their weapons on deck and carried handguns when they went ashore.

Nearly everyone on board the *Snark* suffered from illness or injury all the time. Jack joked that he should call his book about the journey *Around the World in the Hospital Ship Snark*. By the time they made it to Sydney, Australia, Jack was so sick with a tropical fever that he was sent to the hospital for an operation and an extended convalescence. When he did not recuperate as quickly as he hoped, he dosed himself with Salvarsan, which was, according to Stasz, "a toxic arsenic compound that had serious side effects on the kidneys and urinary tract. She adds, "As Jack's physical ailments increased in subsequent years, he looked to the opium derivatives he had learned about in Sydney to bring relief. In his day, he was thought to be acting very sensibly; today, of course, it is known that he was inviting his own destruction."

When Jack was on his feet again, he and Charmian toured Australia and Tasmania, but his illness finally made them decide to end their journey. They sold the *Snark* for a tenth of what it had cost them, and bought steamer tickets for home, reaching Glen Ellen in the middle of July 1909.

In May 1910 Jack bought a seven-hundred-acre vineyard that connected the smaller parcels of land he already owned. He was writing and trying to make his land a model working ranch at the same time, while reconnecting with his old friends of the Crowd.

Charmian typed and edited his manuscripts and tried to cope with the visitors who streamed to Glen Ellen, with or without invitation; after the relative quiet and seclusion of the *Snark*, she found the Crowd's drinking and chatter less congenial than did Jack, who reveled in the company. She found herself feeling ill and out of sorts, and eventually realized she was pregnant. After a difficult labor, she learned that she had had a healthy baby girl but that the doctor had broken her daughter's spinal cord during the delivery; the child lived only thirty-eight hours. (Complications from the botched delivery would cause her to miscarry a second child in 1912; she and Jack had no other children together.)

After the tragic loss of their daughter, the couple turned their attention to the design and building of Wolf House, with the help of Albert Farr, a noted architect. Stasz describes the way Jack conceived of his grand home:

> The house was to be built of local products: redwood, deep chocolate-maroon volcanic rock, blue slate, boulders, and concrete. It would be U-shaped around a large pond (fifteen by thirty feet) filled with mountain stream water and stocked with black bass. The foundation was to be earthquake-proof, its concrete slab strong enough to support a skyscraper. The roof would use the familiar Calforina Spanish tiles, colored specially to harmonize with the maroon of the rock and provide a fireproof cover. . . . Rough-hewn redwood logs would serve as exposed rafters.

Jack's workroom was to be nineteen by forty feet, built over a library the same size. The two-story living room, with redwood balconies from the second floor, would be eighteen by fifty-eight feet, with an immense fireplace. The rooms in the bedroom wing all featured open-air sleeping porches. The most modern conveniences would be found throughout—electric light—a refrigerating room, a vacuum-cleaning plant, a laundry, and storerooms, a root cellar, and a wine cellar would be included in the food-preparation area. His sister Eliza was enlisted to oversee the building of this new home.

As for the working-ranch aspect of his property, his neighbors thought the "city boy" was crazy; his property consisted of six bankrupt ranches where eighteen seasoned farmers had failed to survive financially. This didn't keep him from pouring money into equipment, animals, plants, and ranch hands, so that even though he was making more than seventy-thousand dollars per year—an incredible amount for a young man who had toiled for ten cents an hour at backbreaking labor—he had no cash to spare and most of what he owned was mortgaged.

On August 21, 1913, Jack and Charmian visited the almost-completed Wolf House. They planned to move the next day from the small cottage in which they had been living nearby. That night, Wolf House was burned to the ground. Arson was suspected, but never proved. It was uninsured, and they still owed $100,000 on the house.

DECLINE

Jack had been happy during the years Wolf House was being built; its destruction—and the accompanying financial disaster—sent him into a deep depression. He continued to work, including a stint covering the Mexican Revolution for *Collier's* (at the princely rate of $1,100 per week) until he was disabled by dysentery. He went to Hawaii in 1915 trying to recover his health, but years of hard living, hard drinking, and hard working had taken their toll. In October 1916 his insurance company informed him it was canceling his life insurance policies because of his ill health; the policies had been intended to provide for his daughters, Joan and Becky, in the event of his death. He had put on so much weight that he no longer delighted in physical exercise, and he often drank alcohol to ease the pain of his many ailments.

Still devoted to his ranch, he planned to raise the dam on his property so his artificial lake could irrigate more of his land; he was stunned when his neighbors took him to court over water rights. In November 1916 he testified in court, even though his body was swollen with uremia and he was in great pain. He won the case, but felt bitter toward those who had brought it to court.

On November 21, he rode up into the hills to look at some land he wanted to purchase for its water rights; he returned that evening determined to make an offer to the owner. The following day he was sluggish, rising late and sleeping all afternoon, but full of plans for a school to be built on the ranch when his sister Eliza came by. That night he apparently injected himself with morphine—whether intended to ease his constant pain or to be a lethal dose is debated. When he was found the next morning, a doctor tried to save him, but he remained in a coma and died at 7:45 that evening, November 22, 1916.

CHARACTERS AND PLOT

PLOT

When gold is found near the Klondike River in Canada, men rush to the frozen north, anxious to strike it rich. In order to

35

penetrate the unsettled areas, bring in supplies, and maintain communications, strong dogs are needed to pull dogsleds. The demand for dogs is so high that Manuel kidnaps Buck and sells him to a dog-trader to pay a gambling debt.

For the first four years of his life, Buck has lived a comfortable, dignified life in California, the favorite dog among many, ruler of "this great demesne." Now he is tied and thrust into a train's baggage car by rough men, transported to a strange place where he is sold and caged, then passed along through many hands—none of them kind—on his way north, first to San Francisco, then to Seattle.

In Seattle Buck is turned over to a "dog-doctor," who brutally beats the dog to quickly train him to stop defending himself against men and to obey them as masters. Finally "beaten but not broken," he is bought by Perrault and François to pull sleds delivering Canadian government dispatches; they also buy Curly from the dog-doctor. Men and dogs embark on the ship the *Narwhal*; also on board are Spitz and Dave.

Soon after landing in Dyea, Alaska (located about six hundred miles south of the gold fields, Dyea was one of the closest saltwater ports to the Klondike), Buck watches as Curly makes a friendly approach to a husky dog and is attacked without warning. Thirty or forty dogs run to watch the fight, joining the attack on Curly as soon as she loses her footing and brutally tearing her to pieces. Buck learns not to trust other dogs.

François and Perrault harness Buck and other dogs to a sled. Placed between Dave and Sol-leks, both fair teachers, Buck quickly learns how to respond to the men's commands and how to work with the team. They spend day after day on the trail, nights sleeping in the snow, with Buck always hungry on the slim rations provided. From observing Pike he learns to steal food from the men, feeling no guilt when the clumsier Dub is blamed for his theft. This bit of larceny marks both his ability to adapt and survive and the decay of his "moral nature," which is a handicap in the wilderness. As he becomes lean and fit, his wild heritage comes alive in him; his senses are heightened and he learns or remembers the skills he needs to survive.

Buck hates the lead-dog, Spitz, a hatred formed when he laughed at Curly's fate. They start to fight one miserable night on the trail, but the fight is cut short by an attack on the camp by eighty to one-hundred wild, starving huskies. The two men try to beat back the attackers, but there are too many of them. All nine of the sled dogs are badly injured. They flee for their lives; when they return the next morning, they find that although the men have not been injured, the wild dogs have eaten much of the food and even any leather they could find—sled lashings, a pair of moccasins, part of a whip. Unfortunately, the worst part of their trek lies just ahead. It takes six days to travel the length of Thirty Mile River. Along those thirty miles, Perrault breaks through the ice a dozen times; each time, he is saved by a pole he carries crosswise to keep him from going under the water, but the fifty-degrees-below-zero temperature means he has to stop and build a fire to dry his clothes every time he falls through the ice. Sometimes one or more of the dogs fall through the ice, and the other dogs or the men must pull them from the frigid water. Scaling and descending cliffs may mean that a day's hard labor brings them only a quarter of a mile closer to their goal. Dogs and men come near disaster many times before finally reaching good ice that will reliably bear their weight.

By now, the dogs are all exhausted, but the men push them to make up for lost time. Dolly goes mad from the strain, attacking Buck, and is killed. Spitz seizes the opportunity to attack Buck, and is whipped by François. The hatred between the two dogs deepens, and Buck challenges Spitz for the position as leader of the pack. His insubordination is contagious, destroying the team's solidarity.

One night the team, joined by fifty huskies from a nearby Northwest Police camp, begins chasing a snowshoe rabbit. Buck is leading the pack, his blood lust raging, when Spitz suddenly attacks him. The attacker is the more experienced fighter, but Buck uses his head and defeats his rival, finally killing him.

The next morning, when François tries to put Sol-leks in the lead position, Buck insists the place is rightfully his. After a battle of wills, François gives in and harnesses him in Spitz's old position. With Buck in the lead, the team regains its old solidarity and completes the run in record time.

The team is turned over to a Scotch half-breed to pull a sled in a mail train, a hard and monotonous daily grind with no time to recuperate between runs. Buck does his work well, although he does not like it, and at night by the campfire he dreams of primitive men and ancient times. Dave, who takes pride in his work, is injured or ill, but struggles to keep up; when the men remove him from the harness so he can run alongside, keeping up without having to pull the heavy sled, he begs to be put back in his traces. Finally he cannot keep up at all; after the team has left him behind, one of the men returns to where he lies in the snow and a shot rings out.

After five months, the team has covered 2,500 miles; during the last 1,800 miles, they have had only five days' rest. When they arrive in Skagway, expecting a long rest, the men receive orders to set out again. Since the dogs are in no condition to continue, they are to be sold, while the letter carriers buy new dogs for their next trip.

Hal, Charles, and Mercedes, a family seeking their fortune but woefully unprepared for the rigors of life and travel by dogsled, buy the entire team and supplement it with six untrained dogs. Undisciplined and sloppy, the humans quickly run short of food for the dogs while failing to give them what they need: rest. Dub wrenches his shoulder; untreated, it disables him, and Hal shoots him. The six untrained dogs die from the short rations; Billee and Koona are the next to die. The people quarrel constantly, while the five remaining dogs are little more than skeletons when they stagger into John Thornton's camp at the mouth of the White River. Thornton warns them not to go out onto the ice and Buck senses danger, but Hal whips Buck, trying to force him to move, until Thornton stops him by force. After a brief fight, Thornton cuts Buck's traces.

Hal gives in and leaves Buck behind. While Thornton is checking Buck's wounds, the team and Hal, Charles, and Mercedes fall through the ice and die.

In Thornton's care, Buck recovers, and finds unaccustomed friendship with his dogs, Skeet and Nig. Thornton's kindness and attention awake in Buck a new emotion: love. Warring with this civilized emotion is the pull toward the wild and the primitive; Buck cannot steal from Thornton, but he can still steal from anyone else. He will do anything Thornton asks of him, but at the same time he feels called by the wilderness.

Buck twice saves Thornton's life, once when he is attacked in a bar and again when the man falls into the river and is carried toward the rapids. He proves his worth yet again when Thornton wagers that Buck can pull a sled with a thousand-pound load for a hundred yards. "As you love me, Buck," Thornton asks the dog to pull, and against all odds, the dog succeeds.

Thornton and his partners use the money won in the wager to head east in search of a fabled lost mine. For months they live off the land, searching for the Lost Cabin; although they do not find it, they do find a place rich with gold, which they sack up in fifty-pound bags.

As the men gather gold, Buck again feels the wild calling him from the forest. One night, hearing a timber wolf howl, he goes into the woods to find him. Buck and the wolf become friends, and the two run side by side for hours. Finally Buck remembers Thornton, and slowly returns to his human friend's camp. After two days in the camp, though, he tries to seek out his wolf friend again; although he doesn't find the wolf, he begins staying away from the camp for days at a time, killing his own meat, fishing for salmon, killing a black bear, stalking a moose injured by an arrow. It takes four days to bring down the moose, and he spends another day with his kill, eating and sleeping, before returning to John Thornton.

When he gets back to camp, he finds that Yeehat Indians have killed the men and their dogs and are dancing about the wreckage of the spruce-bough lodge Thornton and his partners had built. Buck attacks the Indians, killing and injuring many of them and forcing the rest to flee in terror. This is the first time he has killed a man; no longer will he fear them unless they are armed.

When night arrives, Buck hears a wolf pack yelping, and goes to join them. They attack him, but are unable to defeat him, while he kills or injures many of them. Finally the pack draws back, and one wolf approaches Buck slowly. When they recognize each other from the day they had spent together, the pack decides to accept Buck.

Now there are wolves that bear markings like Buck's, and the Yeehats tell of a Ghost Dog that runs at the head of the pack, attacking their camps, killing their dogs and hunters, and robbing their traps.

CHAPTER 1

Klondike Adventures

READINGS ON
THE CALL OF THE WILD

The Call of the Wild Recasts Personal Failure as Fictional Triumph

Andrew Sinclair

Jack London's failure to find gold in the Klondike was just the latest in a long string of failures, reports London biographer Andrew Sinclair. London identified himself with Buck, the mistreated hero of *The Call of the Wild*, and poured out a tale that ended in a dog's mastery of the rigors of the Klondike that the man had been unable to achieve. As he fought nightmares that had haunted him since childhood and recorded his fears and deprivations in Buck's bad dreams, London created a work that would finally bring him the success he had long sought.

The gold strike in the Klondike lured [London] to the northland, a way out from the California of wages and workbeasts and failures. Eliza [his half-sister] grubstaked him and her husband to the $500 they needed for their outfits. Their agreement was that the young man would help carry the burdens of the old man. They sailed on the *Umatilla* from San Francisco on July 25, 1897, the boat loaded with gold-seekers, some of the quarter of a million men who were to try their luck at another Eldorado or Bonanza Creek. Of that horde, only 50,000 would reach the interior and 1,000 return richer than they were when they started. But at the beginning of that final westering dream turned northward, who would reckon the waste? . . .

There was something gallant, greedy, and childish in the scramble for the gold of the north. It attracted the visionaries and the failures, the bold and the immature. "There is a

Excerpted from *Jack: A Biography of Jack London* by Andrew Sinclair. Copyright © 1977 by Andrew Sinclair. Reprinted by permission of HarperCollins Publishers, Inc.

splendid uncertainty about the whole affair," Frank Norris wrote, "that invests it with a quality of dignity like a charge of cavalry or a dash for the pole." So the gold-seekers imagined, crammed together on the *Umatilla* and the *City of Topeka* with their outfits, each weighing nearly a ton, littering the decks. Jack was used to the packed masculine society of the forecastle, the conditions were no hardship to him. . . .

His problem was his ailing partner, Captain Shepard, who had suffered a mild heart attack even before they left the dock. He would have to pack the 4,000 pounds of their combined outfits on his own. So he joined forces with three other men on the boats—a small adventurer called Merritt Sloper; a hunter and miner, Big Jim Goodman; and the recorder and cook of the party, thin Fred Thompson with orange whiskers, a man who was both pompous and visionary. Thompson's laconic diary is the tally stick for measuring the myths Jack was to pan from his trip to Alaska. It shows that the party of five reached Juneau in the rain, then paddled onward 100 miles with Indians and hired canoes to Dyea Beach, arriving on August 7. They must hurry on, if they wanted to have a chance of reaching the Klondike before ice made the highland rivers impassable.[1]

The scene at Dyea Beach was a brutal hurly-burly. Thousands of men cursed and struggled with stacks of deadweight stores and crazed horses. Outfits had to be dumped from the dugout canoes onto the shore, then dragged out of the new shanty area. There had only been one shack at Dyea a year before; it would be a ghost town two years later. Meanwhile, all was shouting and trading, with the Siwash Indians of the Tlingit tribes putting up their prices as porters, while the tenderfeet, called *cheechakos*, counted out their money or carried their own stores. Fred Thompson had to pay the Indians 22 cents a pound to have his outfit of 3,000

1. All biographers of Jack London are in the debt of Franklin Walker for his thorough and penetrating book, *Jack London and the Klondike: The Genesis of an American Writer* (London, 1966). He examines in great detail the reality of London's trip to Alaska. For a general appreciation of the phenomenon of the Gold Rush, Pierre Berton's *The Klondike Fever: The Life and Death of the Last Great Gold Rush* (New York, 1958) remains the best account, ably supported by Kathryn Winslow's *Big Pan-Out: The Story of the Klondike Gold Rush* (New York, 1951). In addition to the biographical sources on Jack London, the diary of Fred Thompson of the trip to the Stewart River, and Jack London's own diary and account of the voyage downriver from Dawson City to the sea are essential reading. So are the manuscript memoirs of Emil Jensen and Marshall Bond, the original of which is in the Yale Library. Copies of all these sources are to be found in the Huntington Library (HL).

pounds carried to the summit of the Chilkoot Pass, but the price soon reached 50 cents a pound. A man without money or strength in his shoulders never got beyond Dyea Beach.

A WORK-BEAST AGAIN

So Jack found himself a work-beast again. He had escaped the dumb labor of the laundry only to become his own pack animal over the Chilkoot Pass. . . . Jack and his party . . . hauled their 6 tons of stores on a hired boat upstream to the approach to the pass. After that, they must backpack all the weight up the canyon to Sheep's Camp, then they would have to plod in the Chilkoot lock-step under the threatening glaciers up to the Scales, then finally they needed to perch and cling onto the handholds and toeholds hacked out of the ice on the sheer rocks before the height of the summit, where the squalls and vapors swirled round the human donkeys who had struggled so far.

Jack was strong, but his skin was tender and he had to carry the weight for two men. But luckily Captain Shepard lost his nerve. When the elderly man saw the straining line of gold-seekers on the 14 miles up to the peak of the pass, he complained of a bad attack of rheumatism and turned back for California, leaving Jack to dispose of the spare outfit. His place as cook and packer was soon taken by an old man called Tarwater, who became a mythical Argus in Jack's memories. Although Shepard's going lightened Jack's load, he still had to take up the white man's burden. His belief in the superiority of the Anglo-Saxon race over all others forced him to prove his strength. He was determined to do what the Indians could do, and to do it better.

The heat was so intense on the lower slopes of the Chilkoot that Jack stripped to his underwear and sweated along like a "puffing, steaming, white human engine in scarlet flannels."[2] As, load by slow load, the outfits were lugged up to the summit of the pass, the late August weather changed from sun to cold to driving rain. Underfoot, the dust gave way to the swamp of Pleasant Valley, then to a stretch of brittle tundra leading to broken shale. After these hazards, there was still the fearful bruising of the boulders and the slippery risks of the ice-steps and packed snow of the last trudge to the summit, which the party reached at the end of the month.

2. Charmian London, *The Book of Jack London*, I, p. 228.

All the way from the top of the pass down to the shores of Lake Lindeman ahead, there were abandoned cities of stores, the outfits piled as high as houses, the alleys between them thronged with their despairing owners. To survive the elements of earth and thin air, to lift a ton of food and equipment into the heights, was not enough. The ordeal by water was to come, and it demanded a quick building of boats that could withstand the sudden storms of the lakes and the roaring rapids on the rivers that flowed down to Dawson City. This journey meant death by drowning for the ignorant and an impasse for the unskilled. Jack and Merritt Sloper were both expert in the world of small boats, and the party had brought along its whipsaws and nails, ropes and canvas. There were plenty of spruce trees round Lake Lindeman to provide the timber. Time was the enemy, for the freeze would begin in October. So Jack and his party spent only a fortnight in making their boat, the *Yukon Belle*. They also lent a hand in building a sister ship, *Belle of Yukon*, joining forces with another party that had a woman attached to it. The two boats survived the first passage and portage onto Lake Bennett, where the alternative trail up from Skagway met the Chilkoot trail.

NIGHTMARES AND COURAGE

There Jack saw the confirmation of his dark biological beliefs and nightmares of cruelty. The fate of the horses used on the Skagway trail showed man's inhumanity to his most useful beast as well as to himself. The bodies of hundreds of dead pack animals littered the shores of the lake, shot after they had been flogged almost to death to reach that height. Their carcasses would haunt Jack's Alaskan stories. The tale told Fred Thompson was that there were so many dead horses and mules along the trail, that if they were laid side by side, a man might walk on horseflesh all 50 miles to the lake.[3]

On September 23, the party reached Lake Tagish, where the Canadian customs officials had set up another barrier. By scheming, Jack and his companions only paid little more than $20 tax on their outfits, although many others had their stores confiscated when they could not afford the heavy duties. There were rumors of approaching famine among the

---

3. Fred Thompson's diary, September 21, 1897, *HL*.

immigrants to Dawson City. Those who did not carry 700 pounds of flour and beans and bacon for the winter were turned back. Jack helped old Tarwater to slip through without any provisions, for he had learned to wheedle on the road. Then fair winds took the square-rigged *Yukon Belle* across Lake Marsh to the upper Yukon River, where the first flurries of snow heralded the freeze. The water route now lay through the terrors of Box Canyon.

Many carried their boats for two days round the canyon, while Jack steered the *Yukon Belle* through the rapids in two minutes, then returned to take the next boat through the churning waters. His courage and timing were superb as he stood lashed to the steering oar, riding the hogback of the race, the rock walls dashing by like twin lightning express trains, until the wallowing boat burst through a smoking comber into the whirlpool midway along the canyon, forcing the steersman to ride the curving wall of water onto the second rush of the rapids beyond. Jack repeated his feat 3 miles downriver by taking both boats along the Mane of the White Horse Rapids at racetrack speed. So they reached Lake Laberge. Jack left behind him a myth which he never denied, that he had piloted dozens of boats through the rapids to make a grubstake of $3,000. In fact, he had only done the job twice, the second time out of the kindness of his heart.[4]

A cold north wind nearly stopped the adventurers by the shores of bleak Lake Laberge. It blew for three days. The men must force their stiff bodies and sluggish boat through the thin ice already forming on the lake, or they would have to spend the winter months by that desolate wasteland. Once through, the way down to Dawson City was helter-skelter along the Yukon current. Mush ice was already throwing its broadsides at the *Yukon Belle* from tributary rivers. Even if the sun of an Indian summer broke through the chill dawn fogs, winter was only weeks away, and there were hundreds of miles to travel past shoals and split currents and more rapids and canyons. Anchor ice rose from the river bottom and coated the surface, while the rim ice stretched out its long grip from the cold shore.

After Five Finger Rapids and the 6-mile dash along Rink Rapids, past the trading post at Fort Selkirk where Jack prob-

4. Jack London, "Through the Rapids on the Way to Klondike," *The Home Magazine*, June 1899. Irving Stone states in *Sailor on Horseback* that London earned $3,000 as a steersman at the White Horse Rapids, but the Thompson diary disproves this.

ably saw his first huskies and wolf dogs, a choice had to be made. Old Tarwater transferred to the *Belle of Yukon*, as its crew intended to winter in Dawson City. Jack and his three original companions decided to occupy an abandoned cabin of the Hudson Bay Company on an island at the mouth of the Stewart River, about 80 miles upstream from the city. They were afraid of famine at Dawson and of the high prices there. They were also anxious to begin prospecting, even in the winter. They had come for gold and they meant to stake their claims at once. The Stewart River was said to be a lodestone.

KLONDIKERS' FOLLY

Two days after they had established themselves in their cabin, Big Jim Goodman set out for nearby Henderson Creek to look for likely ground. He returned that same evening with the news that he had struck paydirt. Jack went out with him to the creek, while the other two men prepared the cabin for their winter stay. At the creek, Jack and Goodman panned for gold and staked eight claims. The records in Dawson City still show that Jack London applied for placer mining claim Number 54 on the left fork ascending Henderson Creek, solemnly swearing that he had discovered therein a deposit of "gold."[5]

Although Fred Thompson always maintained that Jack had discovered only fool's gold, his sneer hid his own sense of failure. Modern gold dredges have recovered much of the precious metal from Henderson Creek. What Thompson had to regret was that, like most of the Klondikers, he had wasted his money on the folly of getting there and existing there, taking nothing out. During the rush of 1897 and early 1898, some $60 million was spent on outfits and transport by the gold-seekers, while only $10 million worth of gold was actually grubbed from the soil.[6] By the normal methods of panning, sinking shafts, and sluice mining, the individual miners could only scratch the frozen surface for the metal and break the ground for the professional mining companies, which were to follow with their ore-extracting machines. The story had been the same in California, where the small farmers like John London had only served to clear the

5. See letter of J.D. Dines, Mining Recorder, to Franklin Walker, August 31, 1954, enclosing a copy of Jack London's application for a placer mining claim on November 5, 1897, Franklin Walker Collection, *HL*. 6. See *The American Monthly Review of Reviews*, March 1898.

land for the professional ranchers. The little speculators were the skirmishers of profit, mere cannon fodder for the organized regiments moving in their rear.

ANOTHER EMPTY ILLUSION

Just as the dream becomes the nightmare, the excitement of the rush to the gold became the cold sweat of extracting it. Jack did not mean to break his back at that. Thawing the frozen gravel with spruce fires, sifting the black soil to find occasional grains of the precious metal, were no quicker ways of making money than working in a cannery or a laundry. He had already decided to become a writer, he had already refused to slave as a work-beast. Adventure was one thing, drudgery another. He would not linger for the will-o'-the-wisp of the lucky strike while the body wore down with its hopes. Faced with the dull facts of gold mining, Jack had to recognize another empty illusion. From the waste of his energy and his outfit, he had to pan out the glitter of his struggle, the gleam of some sort of victory over himself. That is why he began to understand the Gold Rush so well. He, too, must soon go home and make a brave show of the last of his series of failures. . . .

[By June 1898] he knew he had failed; his body was in bad shape; he wanted to get back to California as soon as possible.

Jack kept a log of the journey, which he hoped to work into something. He did not think of using the Klondike as a literary asset until he was penniless and leaving it. Yet consciously or unconsciously, he had endured the hard breaking of the tenderfoot by the wilderness, he had listened to the tales of the old-timers. The diary of his voyage downriver was only a postscript to his full memory. . . .

In all, Jack brought home $4.50 worth of gold dust, which he pledged to a pawnbroker in Oakland. He was as broken in health and as penniless as most of the other Klondike adventurers. His only excuse for his folly was the value of the hardship to his character. He must make a myth of his experience, presenting himself as a frail hero who had outlasted the worst of the winter and the wild, not a short-winded young man who had come home with his tail between his legs at the first opportunity. He even believed that the Indians who lived in Alaska could endure the hardship there less well than the white pioneers. They were the necessary victims of the march of civilization. His diary recorded that the "Indian seems unable to comprehend the fact that he can never get the better of the white man." [7]

Jack did not confess that the wilderness had got the better of him, although not of the Indian, nor did he concede that his sense of racial superiority was only a cover for his unspoken failure. The terrible conditions of the Klondike justified his return. "As for the hardship," he wrote later, "it cannot be conveyed by printed page or word of mouth. No man may know who has not undergone. And those who have undergone, out of their knowledge, claim that in the making of the world God grew tired, and when He came to the last barrowload, 'just dumped it anyhow,' and that was how Alaska happened to be." [8]. . .

A BOOK OF NIGHTMARES, FEARS, AND MYTHS

[Four years later, in the winter of 1902–1903] in his home in Piedmont, he did take the time to write his masterpiece, *The Call of the Wild.* The novel is not so much the story of a dog that becomes a wolf as a myth about life and death and nature. It is a saga of the unconscious, written without self-criticism in an age before [psychoanalyst Carl] Jung was known in America. Jack claimed later that he wrote it without any thought about its deeper significance as a human allegory. "I was unconscious of it at the time. I did not mean to do it." [9]

The achievement of the book lies in Jack's fusion of his own suppressed nature with that of a beast. His hero Buck begins as a children's pet, sloppy in the lap of Californian luxury. A kidnapping and a beating by a human demon in a red sweater break Buck's trust in men. As Jack was clubbed into fortune through overwork, Buck is clubbed into the terrible roil of service as a sled-dog in the northern wastes. He transcends his role as a servant of the greed of mankind by reverting to his archetype, the wolf from which he derives. In a fight to the death, he kills the leader of the sled-dogs and becomes the chief of the work-beasts; but his new human masters, as careless of their labor force as any tycoon, make him toil to the edge of extinction. When the love of his saviour

---

7. Jack London, "From Dawson to the Sea," Buffalo *Express*, June 4, 1899. The actual log of the trip down the Yukon is reprinted in full in Charmian London, *The Book of Jack London*, I, pp. 248–257. 8. Jack London, "The Gold Hunters of the North," *Revolution and Other Essays* (New York, 1910), p. 162. See also his article, "The Economics of the Klondike," *The American Monthly Review of Reviews*, January 1900. 9. Quoted in Joan London, *Jack London and His Times*, p. 252.

John Thornton briefly reclaims Buck, it is only an interlude in his descent to the primitive. With Thornton's death at the hands of human savages, Buck becomes the leader of the wolfpack and an avenger upon men, a master of the wilderness. . . .

As Jack called up his unconscious to write his best book, the nightmares of his childhood began again to haunt his life and his work. His dog hero, Buck, had bad dreams, harking back to the life of his forebears. Buck forgot domestication, he lifted his nose to the stars and howled like a wolf at the mystery of the world and the dark and the unknown ages of his inheritance. He dreamed of hairy apish men, his first masters, and he dreamed back to a time of great beasts of prey and total savagery. He also heard the call from the depths of the forest, which filled him with a great unrest and strange desires. He felt a vague, sweet gladness, and yearnings and strivings for he knew not what. His longing for raw meat and blood sent him back to the hunt and the forest. And when his loved master died, he became a spirit of the wild, a ghost dog forever running at the head of the wolfpack, leaping and gigantic, bellowing the song of a younger world.

In Buck's bad dreams, Jack recorded his own childish fears of cold, deprivation, and solitude, as well as his compulsion always to be free and roving, on the hunt to gratify every desire, yet leading his brothers of the wild in the quest of eternal youth. Of course, these were myths—the myth of the birth from nothingness and darkness, the myth of the death of the father in Buck's loved master, and in the pulling down of the bull moose by the pack, the myth of the innocent savage in the wilderness, the myth of the ghost leader forever calling on the young. But Jack believed that people respond to the literature of fear and nightmare, because fear is deep in the roots of the race. However civilized men think they are, fear remains their deepest emotion. In the same period, he had written an essay praising Edgar Allan Poe for his grasp of the terrible and the tragic. He thought the public would respond to his private terror as it did to Poe's own.[10]

10. See Jack London, "The Terrible and Tragic in Fiction," *The Critic*, June 1903.

London Mines Literary Gold from the Klondike

Franklin Walker

Franklin Walker has written a full-length study of London's adventures in the Klondike hoping to strike gold. Although London did not find the "yellow metal," as he calls it in the opening lines of *The Call of the Wild*, he did mine his experiences for a wealth of literary material. Walker examines how London's Klondike experiences were turned into literary gold in his novels and stories, culminating in the enthralling novel about Buck.

In evaluating London's literary output, one must remember that unquestionably he placed substance above form, as did most of his contemporaries. At the threshold of his career he asserted to Elwyn Hoffman: 'After all, it is the substance that counts. What is form? What intrinsic value resides in it? None, none, none—unless it clothe pregnant substance, great substance.'[1] The substance of London's first successful writing was man's experiences in the Far North, together with such comments on his behaviour as seemed appropriate. The Klondike rush was at the heart of the fiction which made him famous. In 1900 he wrote to Con Gepfert, a Stewart River friend who had returned to the Yukon: 'I never realized a cent from any properties I had interest in up there. Still, I have been managing to pan out a living ever since on the strength of the trip.'[2] Earlier he had written to Mabel Applegarth: 'Dig is the arcana of literature, as it is of all things save being born with a silver spoon and going to Klondike.'[3] Failing to inherit the former, he took full advantage of the latter. Through his royalties he was to continue to cash in on a bonanza from the

1. Jack London (hereafter JL) to Elwyn Hoffman, Jan. 6, 1900. HEH (manuscript in Henry E. Huntington Library, San Marino, CA). 2. JL to Con Gepfert, Nov. 5, 1900. Bancroft Library (University of California). 3. JL fragment to Mabel Applegarth, n.d. (probably Jan., 1899). HEH.

Klondike as long as he lived, although his almost exclusive concentration on that field in his writing began to taper off five years after he started washing out his tailings.

The extent to which London's success as a writer, both in the quality of his fiction and the size of his audience, arose from his use of his Yukon experience is well indicated by the extent of his concentration on this field between 1898 and 1903 and his return to it at various times during his later career. . . .

CHARACTERS AND SITUATIONS

An examination of the genesis and development of London's first three volumes of short stories, chronologically arranged, followed by a similar consideration of his Yukon novels, throws valuable light on his use of his Klondike experiences and on his writing techniques. The stories in *The Son of the Wolf* merit particular attention, as they brought him, even in magazine form, a critical acclaim and popular reputation which was to play a vital part in moulding his later fiction. They are held together by their northern settings and by the appearance and reappearance of a group of characters of whom Malemute Kid is the most noteworthy. . . .

The stories of this first volume are laid partly in Yukon settlements like Fortymile during the times antecedent to the Klondike discoveries; partly at Split-up Island, where Malemute Kid has a cabin; partly at Dawson; and frequently on the snowy trail, as in 'The White Silence'. These settings we have already seen in considerable detail. The supporting characters include sourdoughs, who are uniformly hardy and resourceful, and cheechakos, some of whom are brave, like the desperate hero of 'To the Man on Trail', and many of whom are cowardly—misfits and weaklings, clearly unable to adjust themselves to life in the Northland. The plots are not complicated; the tales are usually expanded incidents illustrating certain basic themes. London stated his method succinctly in one of his letters to Con Gepfert. 'I rarely handle plots, but nearly always do handle situations. Take the different ones of my stories which you may recollect, and you will see that they are usually built about some simple but striking human situation.'[4] Ever on the lookout for such situations, London asked Gepfert to send him photos, tell him incidents which he saw or heard about. (He also admit-

4. JL to Gepfert, Nov. 5, 1900. Bancroft Library.

ted that he was aching to return to the Klondike. 'I can hardly contain myself, so strongly do I desire to go back.') . . .

The stories are by no means 'formula' stories nor do they often conform to the editors' demand for a happy ending which London was to cavil at so frequently during his writing career. He advised beginners: 'Avoid the unhappy ending, the harsh, the brutal, the tragic, the horrible—if you care to see in print the things you write. (In this connection don't do as I do, but do as I say.')[5] His writing notes show him constantly searching for situations to illustrate major conflicts faced by man—man against nature, the white man against the Indian, the weak against the strong. A notebook of jottings entitled 'Alaskan Short Story Stuff' contains many such items, with varying degrees of promise:

> 'In a Bear-trap.' [Accompanied by clipping telling of how a man was caught in a trap and finally rescued.] 'Story of Jim Joy': How he loved dance-hall girl, who took all his money and gave him nothing. He is an Indian, and she put it over him dead-easy. Told him to bring more money. He goes out and murders. A story, embodying the Indian point of view and exemplifying the white man's superiority. [This deals with the white man's ability to outpack the Indian.] 'The Joy of Life.' Running with tireless muscles on some adventure through the snow.—Companion to 'The Law of Life.' A story in which a woman, finely bred, leaps upon another and takes away a letter or trinket or token or something from another . . . the animal in her coming to the surface—the panther. . . . A Cooperative society in the Klondyke. The problem of the craze of Gold. The shirkers, and the natural inefficients, arguing that they should all share alike. Road to Dawson. Party of miners. Dude type. Servants with them . . . . In the White Horse rapids they lose almost all their grub . . . . Men show themselves and take control. Put dudes on allowance. Starvation:—finding game and fighting off the hungry men. Look up moose thoroughly. A white woman marries Indian buck—a dashing Indian buck, and her disillusionment. I must write a powerful tale of a man and a wolf-dog. Also a wolf-dog (sort of biographical, like a man), indomitable, fearless, ferocious, and unscrupulous. Build for a scene where he faces a score of antagonists, knowing that they shall tear him to shreds.[6]

ROMANCE AND REALISM

In a letter to Con Gepfert, London explained the emphases he sought in his tales. 'You see, I have had to take liberties,

5. 'Getting into Print', *The Editor*, March, 1903. 6. 'Alaskan Short Story Stuff.' HEH.

and to idealize, etc. etc. for the sake of the artistic effect, and often from the inherent need of the tales themselves, and for their literary value.'[7] In another letter he complained to Gepfert that many Klondikers failed to see the romance in the country. 'Nay, though they live romances, they are not aware of it.'[8] These are vague enough terms; yet one finds on reading London's Klondike stories carefully that, like Martin Eden, he felt a strong turn towards realism, not only in his reliance on scenes and activities which he had experienced, but in his concept of the purpose of fiction. On the use of experience, Martin clearly reflects London's attitude: 'While his imagination was fanciful, even fantastic at times, he had a basic love of reality that compelled him to write about the things he knew.' As to his concept of realism, he felt that he was constantly achieving it by dealing with 'fundamental' conflicts and basically true psychology, nor did he consider that the turn of his plots violated these principles, even though the outcomes might be bizarre.

Never very skilful at articulating his writing attitudes, he fumbles somewhat more successfully in that direction than usual in a letter written to Anna Strunsky. Angered by drastic and partially merited attacks on the accuracy of his portrayal of Indian life, about which he knew very little, he criticized the reviewer, William H. Dall, a well-known authority on North-west Indians, on the grounds that Dall was not an artist and had thus failed to appreciate the reasons for London's selection of details.

> When I have drawn a picture in few strokes, he would spoil it by putting in the multitude of details I have left out. . . . His trouble is that he does not see with a pictorial eye. He merely looks upon a scene and sees every bit of it; but he does not see the true picture in that scene, a picture which can be thrown upon the canvas by eliminating a great mass of things that spoil the composition, that obfuscate the true beautiful lines of it. There is no colour scheme in the scene he sees, no line scheme, no tone scheme, no distribution of light and shading, nothing that may be gained by elimination. He does not understand that mine is not *realism* but is *idealized realism*; that artistically I am an emotional materialist. . . . Further, he has no comprehension of things subjective. Take, for instance, 'In a Far Country.' There the description of the silence, and cold, and darkness, and loneliness, is subjective.[9]

7. JL to Gepfert, May 5, 1900. Bancroft Library. 8. Ibid., Nov. 5, 1900. Bancroft Library. 9. JL to Anna Strunsky, Dec. 20, 1902. HEH. The Dall review was in the *New York Times*, Dec. 6, 1902.

THE ART OF OMISSION

Careful selectivity was an ideal with London, not always easy to achieve. 'The art of omission is the hardest of all to learn, and I am weak at it yet. I am too long-winded, and it is hard training to cut down.'[10] Yet even at the beginning he rarely succumbed to the tendency to pile detail on detail so characteristic of the naturalistic school. Nor did he in these early stories often treat the gruesome and brutal with photographic detail. Though the reviewers pointed out that his tales dealt with 'wild, elemental savagery' and were literature of 'bone and sinew', they found no particular episode or description to object to. The situation might involve the cutting off of a man's head or the eating of a dog; he merely suggested the unpleasant physical activity and did not gloat over it. Sex he treated with even more reticence than the other naturalists of his day. Rare indeed is such a bold remark found as, 'Then he took her in his great arms, and when she tore at his yellow hair laughed with a sound like that of the big bull seal in the rut.'[11] And when S.S. McClure asked him to cut out some swear words, he cheerfully did so, implying that such trivia were of small moment to him. 'Of course I agreed.'[12] In a number of other instances he softened elements in his stories to meet the demands of editors. . . .

SURVIVAL OF THE FITTEST

With *The Children of the Frost* London did better. This volume, made up of ten stories, most of which were published during 1902, concerns itself with Indians or with Indians in contact with whites. The tales are presented from the Indian's point of view. Though they show, as Dall pointed out, very little professional knowledge of the aborigines of Alaska and the Canadian North-west, scarcely discriminating between Indians and Eskimos and differing from the picture of red men elsewhere principally through the emphasis on cold and blubber, they embody effectively two of the themes which London could handle well: the struggle for survival in a primitive environment, and the weakening of a native culture by contact with the predatory Anglo-Saxons. . . .

The best of the stories in *Children of the Frost* are 'The League of the Old Men' and 'The Law of Life'. The former

---

10. JL fragment to Mabel Applegarth (probably Jan., 1899). HEH. 11. *The Son of the Wolf*, p. 225. 12. JL to Johns, Feb. 10, 1900. HEH.

tells of a plot entered into by some old men among the Indians of the upper Yukon to murder all the whites they meet
in camp or on the trail, hoping thereby to discourage the
Anglo-Saxons from coming into the region and thus to prevent the disintegration of their native culture. Of course they
fail, but something of their dignity and tragedy is embodied
in the last survivor, one Imber, who turns himself over to the
law in Dawson City. He tells his story in dramatic terms to a
shocked audience. After a number of killings he has reluc-
tantly come to the conclusion that the newcomers are much
too numerous to be picked off one by one, that they are
much too resourceful to succumb to guerilla tactics, and
that, because they live by the law, they are certain of victory
in the end.

London always affirmed that this was the favourite among
his stories. 'I incline to the opinion that "The League of the
Old Men" is the best short story I have written,' he stated. 'It
has no love-motif, but that is not my reason for thinking it is
my best story. In ways, the motif of this story is greater than
any love-motif; in fact, its wide sweep includes the conditions and situations for ten thousand love-motifs. The voices
of millions are in the voice of old Imber, and the tears and
sorrows of millions are in his throat as he tells his story; his
story epitomizes the whole vast tragedy of the contact of the
Indian and white man.'[13] It is not hard to understand why
London favoured this story, for it combined his sympathy for
the Indians, and underdogs generally, with his belief in the
survival of the fittest through the operation of manifest des-
tiny acting through the Anglo-Saxons. But the story has little
action and less atmosphere; it is too talky to hold its own
with London's best stories.

Much closer to his true forte is 'The Law of Life', which
tells of the approach of death to Old Koskoosh, once an able
warrior, now abandoned in the snow by his tribe to meet the
fate of the decrepit. As the cold moves up and the wolves
close in, he stoically dreams of the old days, particularly of
his experience with a grand old moose who had eventually
been forced to give up just as he was doing.

This story is told effectively by a writer who had learned
a great deal about his craft in two years. In a letter to
Cloudesley Johns, London used it to illustrate points he

13. 'My Best Short Story,' *The Grand Magazine* (London), Aug., 1906. MS in HEH.

wished to make about universality, objectivity, and control of point of view in writing.

> It is short, applies the particular to the universal, deals with a lonely death, of an old man, in which beasts consummate the tragedy. My man is an old Indian, abandoned in the snow by his tribe because he cannot keep up. He has a little fire, a few sticks of wood. The frost and silence about him. He is blind. How do I approach the event? What point of view do I take? Why, the old Indian's, of course. It opens up with him sitting by his little fire, listening to the tribesmen breaking camp, harnessing dogs, and departing. The reader listens with him to every familiar sound; hears the last draw away; feels the silence settle down. The old man wanders back into his past; the reader wanders with him—thus is the whole theme exploited through the soul of the Indian. Down to the consummation, when the wolves draw in upon him in a circle. Don't you see, nothing, even the moralizing and generalizing, is done, save through him, in expressions of his experience.[14]

In 'The Law of Life' the Indian was forced to accept the principle that: 'Nature was not kindly to the flesh. She had no concern for that concrete thing called the individual. Her interest lay in the species, the race.' In this way London continued to dramatize his interpretation of Darwin, feeling that here the biological theory of survival of the fittest applied to the extinction of the moose and the old man just as in 'The League of the Old Men' it applied to the success of the virile, imaginative races like the Anglo-Saxons, 'the salt of the earth', as he liked to call them. He wedded Darwin and Kipling in this fashion—not as difficult a union to manage as the union of Darwin and Marx, effected in his later fiction by assuming that the survival of the fittest applied to classes as well as to individuals and that the proletariat was the class most fit to survive.

CLOAKING IDEAS IN FICTION

In these early stories as in almost all his fiction, London embodied his ideas in his action. He was particularly impressed with social and economic theories and felt that their exposition was an important function of the novelist. As he stated in 'The Material Side', a writer can present his ideas, and still make a living, by cloaking them in fiction which appeals mainly through its story line. Of messages, 'we will weave them about with our fictions, and make them beautiful, and

14. JL to Johns, Dec. 22, 1900. HEH.

sell them for goodly sums.'[15] In another article he urged every writer to develop a significant 'Philosophy of Life', a condition to be achieved by reading intelligently. He made no attempt to hide the enthusiasms he developed from what he called his 'collateral reading'. To Anna Strunsky he remarked, quite appropriately, 'The influences at work in me, from Zangwill to Marx, are obvious.'[16] There is much Darwin, Huxley, and Spencer in his Klondike fiction but surprisingly little Marx, considering the fact that he had for several years been an enthusiast for Marx. Nor was Nietzsche to leave any strong mark on his Yukon books; the latter was to play no prominent part in his writing until *The Sea-Wolf* in 1904. In the Klondike books, he was as good an imperialist as the rest; he praised predatory business methods in *A Daughter of the Snows* and elsewhere seemed unconcerned about the plight of the poor. The element in his nature which in the final analysis brought together all these seemingly incompatible elements from his reading and experience—the genuine sympathy with the dispossessed native, the pride in the predatory Anglo-Saxon, the enthusiasm for the revolt of the masses—was his joy in conflict, his feeling that the persecuted must fight, his admiration for the fighter that could win.

THE CALL OF THE WILD

This glory in fighting to hold one's own came to its climax and most satisfactory expression in *The Call of the Wild*, London's second novel. . . .

The Call of the Wild . . . started out as a short story and ended up a novel. Not long before he began Buck's narrative, London had written a tale which he entitled 'Bâtard', but which the prudent *Cosmopolitan* had altered to 'Diable: a Dog', to spare their readers' sensibilities. It told of a bitter feud between a mongrel dog and his vicious master which ended in the dog killing the man. London confided to Anna Strunsky that his new dog story started out as a companion piece to this tale: 'I started it as a companion to my other dog-story, "Batard", which you may remember; but it got away from me, and instead of 4000 words it ran 32000 before I could call a halt.'[17] It was the story of a very different dog from Bâtard, a 'civilized' dog, a cross between a St Bernard and a sheep dog, which was stolen from his home in

---

15. 'The Material Side,' *Junior Munsey Magazine*, Dec., 1900. 16. JL to Anna Strunsky, Jan. 21, 1900. HEH. 17. JL to Anna Strunsky, March 13, 1903. HEH.

California and taken north to the Klondike, where he became a superior sled dog under the tutelage of a kind master, Thornton.

The two principal themes in the book were almost perfect reflections of London's thinking of this period. The animal's struggle to adjust to his new life as a sled dog brings out every element of adaptability, resourcefulness, and grit which Buck possesses. In coping with men and dogs, he learns to defend his rights and then thrusts on until he is a leader. With no more training to make him a good sled dog than London had had to be a writer, he uses brains and brawn to win his way. He is, of course, Jack London making his effort to be successful, to win in the fight, and to be loved, particularly in the episodes dealing with Thornton. The second theme, that of atavism, arose partly because of London's interest in evolution, partly through the pervasive wildness of the far northern lands. The idea of going backward in the evolutionary process appealed widely at this time. Note, for instance, Frank Norris' 'Lauth', in which he has a human being 'devolve' through various stages of animal life until he becomes nothing but a mass of protozoa. Buck dreams more and more of his wild dog ancestors and the primitive experiences of his kind. Eventually, after Thornton's death, he joins a wolf pack to live in the forest and howl under the stars for the rest of his life.

But the concept of 'the call of the wild' was not solely a reflection of the atavistic ideas arising from popular interest in the Darwinian theory. The part of Buck that was Jack London was escaping from the confining elements in society. For the contemporary reader, the 'call' represents the tug on all civilized men to get away from routine tasks, to simplify their lives in somewhat the same way Thoreau wanted them simplified, to find adventure in nature far from cities and family responsibilities. It is because *The Call of the Wild* is one of the great victory and escape books in American literature that it has continued to be read by old and young. It is filled with soul-satisfying action in a setting which London handles vividly, carefully, and memorably.

The Call of the Wild Is an Early Example of Modern Sociobiology

James Lundquist

The months London spent in the Klondike during the height of the gold rush were a "Darwinian nightmare," in the words of James Lundquist. By the time London left the Klondike, writes Lundquist, he had conceived of that savage territory as a laboratory where men must learn the laws of survival. Yet, while the ideas of eugenics and selective breeding were popular science at the time, London's attitudes and beliefs, as shown in *The Call of the Wild*, anticipated today's emphasis on sociobiology, which examines the biological basis of social behavior. In addition to his study of London, Lundquist has written books on several other literary figures, including J.D. Salinger, Kurt Vonnegut, and Chester Himes.

London devoted so many pages to the great gold rush of 1897 and talked about it so much in his lectures that accounts of his supposed exploits—such as shooting the Mane of the White Horse Rapids—are still being told in the saloons of Dawson, and more than one old-timer over the years has claimed to be his long-lost son. But as willing as London always was to profit from the romantic lore that made him out to be so much more than he actually was—for the most part, just another sourdough who spent a miserable winter on Split-Up Island— he had no illusions about his Klondike stories. He did not write them as documentary narratives; he wrote them as meditations on what happens to men and beasts when they are thrust into "the Wild, the savage, frozen-hearted Northland Wild," as he terms it in *White Fang*.

The Northland, as London experienced it from the moment

he set foot on Dyea beach, was a Darwinian nightmare. The screaming horses, the arguments over tangled gear, the fist-fights, and the distant sound of scores being settled with drawn revolvers could only have confirmed the evolutionary survival-of-the-fittest theories that were already embedded in his deepest consciousness. Within a few days he and his part-ners were reduced to pack animals as they lugged and sweated their outfits up and over Chilkoot Pass. Their journey through the lakes and rivers to Dawson seemed to be taking them to the "unprotected tip of the planet," and that winter London would lie on his bunk in a tiny cabin at the conflu-ence of two frozen rivers and think about the sudden death that waited for him at seventy-five degrees below zero just outside the door. His respect for the men who could actually thrive in such an environment gradually overwhelmed his imagination. He began to see them as emblematic figures who had somehow developed a code of behavior that would enable them to endure life at the very limits of existence. Some of these men he had met at the Moosehorn Bar and the Elkhorn Saloon in Dawson the previous fall, men with nick-names like "Slackwater," "Siwash," and "Axe-handle." Others had stopped for a rest at Split-Up Island, where they accepted steaming mugs of tea and told stories about running the "Salt-water Mail" to Skagway with wolves howling around them all the way. The wolves themselves were topics of conversation, as were the sled dogs the mushers talked about as if each dog possessed a human personality. London may even have heard a tale about a giant husky that had gone wild and turned into a "Ghost Dog."

London did not spend much time—if any—working his claim on Henderson Creek. And as far as is known, he did not do any writing until he began the diary he kept of his float down the Yukon on his way out. But when he returned to Oakland and began to compose the cycle of Northland stories that begins with "To the Man on Trail" and culminates in *The Call of the Wild,* he had developed a vision of the Klondike as an enormous laboratory of red-blooded adventure, where his characters could be reduced to "primordial simplicity" as they learn the frostbitten truth about the Law of Life. Survival for both man and beast in such an environment depended on the successful adoption of instinctive codes of behavior that often obscured the differences between men and animals.

As London thought about what he had heard and seen in the

Northland, the nicknamed men of the Dawson saloons worked their way through his imagination and emerged as the Malemute Kid and Sitka Charley. The Ghost Dog turned into Buck, and out of the wolf pack came White Fang. These characters exist to teach the essential lesson that runs through all of the Klondike stories: "When a man journeys into a far country, he must be prepared to forget many of the things he has learned, and to acquire such customs as are inherent with existence in the new land; he must abandon the old ideals and the old gods, and oftentimes he must reverse the very codes by which his conduct has hitherto been shaped."[1] . . .

SOCIAL BEHAVIOR OF ANIMALS

The science of eugenics was part of fashionable biology at the turn of the century, and it was one London's major interests. London even wrote a letter to the *Medical Review of Reviews* in 1910 expressing his belief that the human future would be determined by the practice of selective breeding.[2] Although this notion appears to be but one more example of London's obsession with Anglo-Saxon racial superiority, it reveals how central the relationship between animal and human behavior was to his thought and to his fiction. On this score, his ideas now appear to be much more in line with the new hybrid science of sociobiology than they do with the primitive eugenic theories of his era, as can be seen in *The Call of the Wild* and *White Fang.*

London's main reputation as a novelist continues to depend on his two best-known dog books. And his tendency to see himself as part animal—he signed his intimate letters "Wolf," named his mansion "Wolf House," owned a husky called "Brown Wolf," and had a wolf's head as a bookplate—has been interpreted as an all-too-apparent statement of personality by psychologists. London was, however, thoroughly devoted to the ideas of Darwin and Spencer, and this involved more than the idea of the survival of the fittest or his own conception of himself as a predatory beast. Many of his statements about the relationship between humans and animals anticipate those of such recent writers as E.O. Wilson in his 1975 book *Sociobiology: The New Synthesis.* Wilson, regarded as the father of the new science, and other sociobiologists

1. Jack London, "In a Far Country," in *Novels and Stories,* The Library of America (New York: Viking, 1982), p. 308. 2. Jack London to Frederick H. Robinson, September 5, 1913, *Letters from Jack London,* edited by King Hendricks and Irving Shepard (New York: Odyssey Press, 1965), p. 398.

make a case for "the systematic study of the biological basis of all social behavior."[3] Like Wilson, London stresses the importance of applying insights gained from the social behavior of animals (and sometimes even insects) to the study of human nature. London's writings on the subject are more in the spirit of the ethology later popularized by Konrad Lorenz, Robert Ardry, and Desmond Morris, and he knew nothing about the notion of the gene as the unit of evolution, which is what makes sociobiology such a radical departure in the study of animal behavior. Nevertheless, in one prophetic essay, "The Other Animals," published in *Collier's* for September 1908, and included in *Revolution and Other Essays* (1910), London defends himself against a charge of "nature faking" and at the same time sets forth his own understanding of the differences between human and animal thought processes.

A PROTEST AGAINST HUMANIZING ANIMALS

The essay, which should be read as a preface to all of London's dog stories, was written in response to President Theodore Roosevelt's attack, in a 1907 interview, on London's depiction of certain episodes in *White Fang* when a bulldog and a lynx both fight a wolf-dog. Roosevelt's specific objections now seem superficial (indeed, he misread the novel on one point), but his concluding remarks reiterated a long-standing criticism of London's accuracy in his Northland stories. "Men who have visited the haunts of the wild beasts, who have seen them, and have learned at least something of their ways," said Roosevelt, "resent such falsifying of nature's records."[4] After pointing out that the President was wrong in the "field observations" he took while reading the book, and stating that whether a "bull-dog can lick a wolf-dog" or not is simply a difference of opinion, London begins his essay by explaining that *The Call of the Wild* and *White Fang* were written partly as a protest against the "humanizing" of animals by other writers.

London flatly states that he believes dogs can indeed think, but that they are "not directed by abstract reasoning, but by instinct, sensation, and emotion, and by simple reasoning." He emphasizes that at all points he has endeavored to keep

3. E.O. Wilson, *Sociobiology: The New Synthesis* (Cambridge, Mass.: Harvard University Press, 1975), p. 41. 4. Reprinted as "Men Who Misinterpret Nature," in Theodore Roosevelt, *The Winning of the West: The Works of Theodore Roosevelt* (New York: H. Holt, 1924–26), p. 4.

his work in line with the facts of evolution, and that the idea put forth by the President—that man is the only animal capable of reason—is "distinctly medieval." London agrees that many animal responses are fixed in species through adaptation to environment; however, he objects to the idea that an animal cannot successfully adjust to a strange environment for which heredity has not provided an adjustment. Using observations of "rudimentary reason" in dogs he has owned, he attacks the idea of homo-centricity by pointing out that the theory of evolution must include the evolution of reason—a theory that recognizes no impassable gulfs from species to species. "Let us be very humble," London cautions. "We who are so very human are very animal." We cannot deny our "relatives, the other animals," because their history is our history. "What you repudiate in them, you repudiate in yourself—a pretty spectacle, truly, of an exalted animal striving to disown the stuff of life out of which it is made," London writes, "striving by use of the very reason that was developed by evolution to deny the processes of evolution that developed it. This may be good egotism, but it is not good science."

London was not a scientist, of course, and made a number of mistakes in describing animal behavior. He has been criticized most severely for his representation of wolves as savage beasts which inevitably track his characters across the snow-fields and gather in a circle around them, waiting for the campfire to go out. Recent studies have shown that wolves are in fact terrified by human beings, and L. David Mech in his book *The Wolf* goes so far as to argue that "In North America, no scientifically acceptable evidence is available to support the claim that healthy wild wolves are dangerous to man.[5] London, along with most who were with him in the Klondike, would have stared in disbelief at anyone who would make such a statement. To be certain, London's concept of the wolf comes out of ancient folklore and superstition that was still very much accepted fact when he was writing. It is true, as Barry Lopez writes in *Of Wolves and Men*, that London's novels "show a preoccupation with 'the brute nature' in men, which he symbolized in the wolf."[6] But London carefully worked out his theories of animal behavior, and he repeatedly pointed out that the dogs and wolves in his stories are not to

5. L. David Mech, *The Wolf* (Garden City, N.Y.: Natural History Press, 1970), p. 291. 6. Barry Lopez, *Of Wolves and Men* (New York: Scribners, 1978), p. 218.

be taken as literary representations of human types dressed up in fur coats.

A DIFFERENT KIND OF NATURALISM

London, in his emphasis on "rudimentary reason" and his objection to "humanizing" animals, made a clear distinction between his books and the earlier animal books—Anna Sewell's *Black Beauty* (1877), Rudyard Kipling's *Jungle Book* (1894), and Ernest Thompson Seton's *Wild Animals I Have Known* (1898)—that have sometimes been seen as influences on him. He knew the books, understood the reasons for their popularity, and was trying to capitalize on their success. At the same time, nevertheless, he was presenting a much tougher-minded interpretation of animal behavior and what it can teach us about human nature. Unlike Sewell, London never tries to make us feel sorry for his animals. Unlike Kipling, London never has his animals speak with human voices. And unlike Seton, London does not try to show the essential nobility of animals as an argument for the wilderness-preservation movement.

The term "naturalism" has often been used in reference to London's emphasis on sociological and biological determinism, his belief in the materialistic nature of man, and his reliance on the survival-of-the-fittest thesis; and London is usually classified with Frank Norris and Theodore Dreiser as a "naturalistic" writer. But London's naturalism must be understood in a somewhat different way, in reference to his dog books and his role as a literary precursor of sociobiology. To London, man and animals are similar in most aspects of behavior because all species must live under the Law of Life, which is to say they are all subject to the processes of evolution. Under stress—such as in the Klondike stories—both man and beast must develop methods of survival based on a combination of adaptability and instinct. Some adapt successfully, some revert atavistically, and some perish. But the Law is the same for all, as *The Call of the Wild* and *White Fang* ferociously illustrate. . . .

NOT JUST ANY DOG STORY

The enormous attention *The Call of the Wild* brought London is often attributed to its subject. As George Jean Nathan remarked, "In the many years of my incumbency as a magazine editor, it was a general, and occasionally embarrassing fact, that any even half-way good dog story usually attracted wider attention among the readers—and certainly a lot more enthusiastic letters to the editor—than almost anything else."[7]

But *The Call of the Wild* is not just any dog story. London departs from the traditional depictions of dogs in fiction at almost every point. Buck is not cute, he is not gentle, and he does not do clever tricks; at one point he learns to steal, and by the end of the novel he has turned into a killer. Everything he does, he does as London thought a dog actually would. All of his thinking is presented as dog thoughts. And when he begins to respond to his primordial instincts, he does so as a dog, not as a man. It is London's "dog psychology" that contributes the most to the unique effect of the novel and what also makes a lot of critical terminology essentially useless in dealing with it—as well as with much of London's other work. Given the plain, narrative fact that London is showing us a dog as he thinks dogs are, it becomes absurd to refer to Buck as completing "rites of passage" or indulging in "ritualistic acts." This is not to say that *The Call of the Wild* is not an extremely literary novel. The recurring use of the color white, particularly in the scene when Buck and Spitz and the rest of the dogs chase the snowshoe hare, brings *Moby-Dick* to mind. And the relationship between John Thornton and Buck is suggestive of *Huckleberry Finn.* Thornton frees Buck from slavery and learns much about steadfastness and love from him, even though Buck is a "lower" creature, just as Huck learns from Nigger Jim. London's twist, of course, is that it is Buck who lights out for the territory at the end, showing that London, well read as he was, wanted his own way with his own material.

The wonderfully lyric description of Buck's journey with Thornton and his partners in search of the fabled lost gold mine has been interpreted as a "quest" leading to "rites of sacrifice" or "rites of succession" involving totemic animals. But such an approach needlessly complicates the story. In London, atmosphere is sometimes all, and he simply tells us that "In the fall of the year they penetrated a weird lake country, sad and silent, where wild-fowl had been, but where there was no life nor sign of life—only the blowing of chill winds, the forming of ice in sheltered places, and the melancholy rip-

7. George Jean Nathan, *The Theatre Book of the Year, 1942–43* (New York: Knopf, 1943), p. 68.

pling of waves on lonely beaches." The imagery alone makes the conclusion of the novel take on its own justification. Thornton and his partners do strike it rich, but the primitive Yeehats kill them, and the even more primitive Buck kills the Indians, thus passing into aboriginal legend as the "Ghost Dog," indeed becoming totemic to the Indians. Still, to London, Buck remains a dog, capable of rudimentary reason but driven by instinct, running "side by side with the wild brother, yelping as he ran." As London warns in his opening sentence, "Buck did not read the newspapers."

London Advances Cruel and Incorrect Fantasies of the Animal World

John Perry

London makes his story of barbarity, hostility, and a neurotic fixation with man's brute nature acceptable to some readers by wrapping them in a dog's disguise, asserts John Perry. Perry, author of the biography *Jack London: An American Myth*, from which this viewpoint is taken, charges that even London's cruel fantasies of the animal world are wrong; for example, wolves are really afraid of humans, unlikely to attack as London's furry characters do. Perry has also written a book on nineteenth-century American dramatist James A. Herne.

Why did *The Call of the Wild* become a phenomenal best-seller? To answer this is to answer the success of Mother Goose or Kahlil Gibran. Chance played a key role in London's jackpot novelette. Macmillan's massive push also planted seeds in the public's mind. Its subject matter—dogs—helped a lot. "In the many years of my incumbency as a magazine editor, it was a general, and occasionally embarrassing, fact that any even halfway good dog story usually attracted wider attention among the readers," recalled George Jean Nathan, "and certainly a lot more enthusiastic letters to the editor—than almost anything else, however highly creditable to the art of belles-lettres, in the particular issue."[1] In *The Call of the Wild: 1900–1916*, a study of American culture between 1900 and 1916, Roderick Nash offers another reason for Buck's bonanza:

> In the case of *The Call of the Wild* the significance is comparatively clear. The book is an allegory; it deals with dogs

1. George Jean Nathan, *The Theatre Book of the Year 1942–1943* (New York: Alfred A. Knopf, 1943), p. 68.

but pertains to men. In describing Buck's progress from tameness to wildness, the author passed judgment on his contemporaries. They too, he implied, suffered from over-civilization, and in the early 1900s the idea struck a sympathetic chord. For many the growth and change of the United States over the previous hundred years seemed to have brought not the millennium once expected but rather a state of confusion, corruption, and debilitating abundance. For such people, Buck's simple, vigorous, unrestrained life in the North was very appealing. As the twentieth century dawned, the nation found itself drawn toward virility, toward novelty, toward nature. Significantly, London's *White Fang* (1906) in which a wolf became a family dog, never enjoyed the popularity of *The Call of the Wild*.[2]

SAVAGE LAW

The Call of the Wild . . . opens on a restful note, Buck living "at a big house in the sun-kissed Santa Clara Valley. Judge Miller's place it was called.". . . (The real-life Buck belonged to Louis Bond, someone London knew at Dawson during the gold rush, and Louis's father, Judge Bond, owned the Santa Clara Valley ranch.) Reading into the story, one soon realizes that Buck symbolizes Jack London's Anglo-Saxon theories and harsh racist views. Buck lives "the life of a sated aristocrat" on the ranch, having "a fine pride in himself, was ever a trifle egotistical, as country gentlemen sometimes become because of their insular situation." He's "king over all creeping, crawling, flying things of Judge Miller's place, humans included," something especially true regarding "Toots, the Japanese pug, or Ysabel, the Mexican hairless,—strange creatures that rarely put nose out of doors or set foot to ground."[3]

Instead of evolving according to the progressivism of Herbert Spencer and Benjamin Kidd, Buck regresses, both morally and socially, London hinting this in the novelette's prefatory poem: "Old longings nomadic leap, / Chafing at custom's chain; / Again from its brumal sleep / Wakens the ferine strain." When conditions awaken primitive instincts, civilization's surface veneer vanishes, leaving an atavistic brute who survives through raw physical strength. This happens to Buck through Manuel, a gardener's helper on the Miller ranch, who kidnaps the "high-strung and finely sen-

2. Roderick Nash, ed., *The Call of the Wild: 1900–1916* (New York: George Braziller, 1970), p. 2. 3. Jack London, *The Call of the Wild* (New York: Macmillan Co., 1903), pp. 18–19, 18.

sitive" dog, selling him to money-grubbers as a Klondike sled dog. The trusting Buck, thrown into the primitive, soon learns a big lesson: "that club was a revelation. . . . A man with a club was a lawgiver, a master to be obeyed, though not necessarily conciliated."[4] Pain teaches this lesson. Thereafter Buck avoids the club through cunning and dominance of weaker creatures, leaving them to suffer his savage abuses and exploitations.

Two French-Canadians, Perrault and François, eventually buy Buck, taking him to the Yukon. . . . London sketches these half-breeds sympathetically, particularly François, who makes moccasins for Buck's sensitive feet, saves him several times from the treacherous dogs, and weeps when they part. Buck learns fast in this white wilderness. "They were savages, all of them, who knew no law but the law of club and fang." When the gentle Curly, "a good-natured Newfoundland," is devoured alive, "screaming with agony beneath the bristling mass of bodies," the second law is implanted on Buck's sharp mind: "So that was the way. No fair play. Once down, that was the end of you. Well, he would see to it that he never went down."[5] The dog Spitz, who laughs at Curly's horrible end, becomes the archenemy of Buck, each waiting for a chance to kill the other.

Once Buck realizes what operates on Yukon ice, he becomes a thief, stealing to live in this "dog eat dog" world on the edge of civilization, where one needs strength, imagination, and the ability to adapt to changing environmental conditions, something Curly lacked. Violent death becomes the ultimate fate of inferiors. As the narrator says in "The Wisdom of the Trail," "I, I, I, want to exist!—the dominant note of the whole living universe."[6] So Buck becomes a bully, an agitator who undermines "the solidarity of the team. . . . it was a greater delight slyly to precipitate a fight amongst his mates and tangle the traces." When he finally kills Spitz, he realizes that "mercy was a thing reserved for gentler climes. . . . Buck stood and looked on, the successful champion, the dominant primordial beast who had made his kill and found it good."[7]

As Buck's muscles toughen through the toil of traces, his sense of morality weakens, while instincts strengthen. Past

4. Ibid., pp. 15, 25, 32, 33. 5. Ibid., pp. 43, 34–37, 45, 45. 6. Jack London, *Son of the Wolf* (Boston: Houghton Mifflin, 1900), p. 147. 7. Jack London, *Call of the Wild*, pp. 89, 98, 99.

harkings of the forests primeval begin to possess his will. "The domesticated generations fell from him. In vague ways he remembered back to the youth of the breed, to the time the wild dogs ranged in packs through the primeval forest and killed their meat as they ran it down. It was no task for him to learn to fight with cut and slash and the quick wolf snap. In this manner had fought forgotten ancestors."[8]

GLORIFYING THE PRIMITIVE

. . . "The philosophy of *The Call of the Wild* consists in a glorification of sheer strength and cunning," writes Walter Fuller Taylor. "London's hero is—insofar as human traits can be attributed to a dog—a savage individualist, exulting with the strength of the strong in the struggle for existence, fighting his way to mastery with the ruthlessness of the dominant primordial brute."[9] Philo C. Buck, who wrote a scathing essay in the *Methodist Review* on London, called him "The American Barbarian," saying: "He is an atavism. But it is this very return to the primitive in the present, like the romantic stories of the strenuous day of the past, that arouses the enthusiasm of hero-worshiping youth. It is this that explains the huge popularity of such stories as *The Sea Wolf, The Call of the Wild, Burning Daylight*, and even *Martin Eden*. Their 'elemental strength,' as a critic phrases it, their war against the conventions of society, their love of combat, their delight in pure physical existence—in a word, their essential barbarity is cause sufficient for their magnetic hold upon our imaginations."[10]

While Buck dreams about hairy cavemen and senses nature's primal call of the wild, he passes through the hands of several more masters, including a Scotch half-breed, then three tinhorns—Hal, Charles, and Mercedes, all symbolic of decadent civilization. These losers first feed the dogs too much, then too little, and Mercedes—another of London's weak-minded women—adds to the dogs' exhaustion by riding on the sleigh. When her husband and brother remove her, "she let her legs go limp like a spoiled child, and sat down on the trail. . . . And through it all Buck staggered along at the head of the team as in a nightmare." They finally reach the mouth of White River, where John Thornton cuts

8. Ibid., p. 62. 9. Walter Fuller Taylor, *A History of American Letters* (New York: American Book Company, 1936), p. 317. 10. Philo S. Buck, "The American Barbarian," *Methodist Review*, 94 (1912), p. 718.

Buck's traces, forcing them to continue without him. When a section of ice collapses, they're killed, vanishing into the Yukon's yawning jaws, their terrible death ignored by John Thornton, who merely looks at Buck, saying: "You poor devil."[11] And Buck licks his hand.

John Thornton becomes Buck's ideal master, London calling this chapter "For the Love of Man." Written from Buck's point of view, however, the true nature of Thornton, another London "hairy" loser, becomes blurred. (In one paragraph he repeats the word "hairy" five times, stressing the man's primitivism, saying he "seemed as much at home among the trees as on the ground." Like Hans and Pete, his two partners, Thornton lives close to nature, a clear thinker unafraid, yet accident-prone like London. . . . Buck saves him twice, once from Black Burton in a barroom knockdown, the second time from rapids, both courageous canine acts of devotion. But Thornton shows thoughtless concern for Buck, once asking him to jump off a cliff, a command the dog begins to obey. Reduced to their last two hundred dollars, Thornton and his partners hope to win sixteen hundred dollars, boasting Buck could do the impossible: start a thousand pounds on a frozen sled. Buck achieves this torturous feat, of course, as Thornton follows the sled, "cursing Buck, and he cursed him long and fervently, and softly and lovingly."[12] (London based the sled race on an actual happening, detailed in "Husky—The Wolf Dog of the North" [*Harper's Weekly*, June 30, 1900].)[13]

Greedy for gold and using the $1,600, the three men start east "after a fabled lost mine," spending nearly two years tracing it, then luckily find "a shallow placer in a broad valley where the gold showed like yellow butter across the bottom of the washing pan." While Buck runs free through the forests, "a killer, a thing that preyed, living on the things that lived, unaided, alone by virtue of his own strength and prowess, surviving triumphantly in a hostile environment where only the strong survived," Yeehat Indians surprise the three men, who failed to post a guard, and slaughter them. Returning to camp, satiated with nature's throbbing call that takes him into the wild for longer and longer periods, Buck scatters the Indians, killing several, which possesses him

11. Jack London, *Call of the Wild*, pp. 144, 145, 157. 12. Ibid., pp. 189, 198–99. 13. Jack London, "Husky—The Wolf-Dog of the North," *Harper's Weekly*, 44 (1900), p. 611.

with an exhilarating sense of ecstasy: "He had killed man, the noblest game of all, and he had killed in the face of the law of club and fang. He sniffed the bodies curiously. They had died so easily. It was harder to kill a husky dog than them. They were no match at all, were it not for their arrows and spears and clubs."[14]

His ties severed with civilization, Buck becomes a legendary Ghost Dog, an Evil Spirit, creating a superior strain of animal by mating with a wolf. (This, of course, contradicts London's theory that crossbreeds perpetuate inferior stock.) London ends *The Call of the Wild* with his most famous lines: "But he is not always alone. When the long winter nights come on and the wolves follow their meat into the lower valleys, he may be seen running at the head of the pack through the pale moonlight or glimmering borealis, leaping gigantic above his fellows, his great throat a-bellow as he sings a song of the younger world, which is the song of the pack."[15]

THE ANIMAL SIDE OF HUMAN NATURE

London's absorption with nature's "dominant primordial beasts," his work roving between the worlds of romance and raw primitivism, borders on the ridiculous, the kind of thing H.L. Mencken called "muck for the multitudes." This even mars *The Call of the Wild*, in which Buck dreams about a caveman sitting around an ancient fire, sometimes scurrying up trees for protection from wild beasts. . . .

Why London's interest in cavedom? It certainly didn't embrace the period's "return to nature" talk, an American pipe dream since the time of Thoreau. Perhaps *The Bookman* explained: "It is the animal side of human nature that Mr. London always delights in exalting, in all the relations of life."[16] In such a woeful world, man's fighting instinct dominates, so does human depravity. Ethics become absurd, man's assurance of broken bones and starving stomachs. Primitivism also negates the spine of Herbert Spencer's credo that humanity evolves, not devolves. Regression, of course, spells out decay, another central London theme, from Alaska's white wilderness to the decayed tropical vegetation of South Sea islands—a peculiar slant during America's strenuous age of Rooseveltian virility and optimism.

14. Jack London, *Call of the Wild*, pp. 193, 197, 207, 223. 15. Jack London, *Call of the Wild*, pp. 228–31. 16. "The Dearth of Ideas and Some Recent Novels," *The Bookman*, 38 (September–February 1913–1914), p. 542.

The period's literary preoccupation with European naturalism, which often reduced men to wild, elemental beasts, provided a popular framework for London's primitivism. . . .

[His view was] stated in such articles as "The Somnambulists"[17] that beneath the skin, man and beast share common inheritances. Remove civilized man to a remote region? He's soon reduced to an elemental force, devoid of values, stalking food to survive. "Morals are not the important thing, nor enlightenment—nor civilization," said Mark Twain. "A man can do absolutely well without them, but he can't do without *something to eat.* The supremest thing is the needs of the body, not of the mind & spirit."[18] London illustrates this in "Bâtard, a Dog." It also happens to the peaceful Buck in *The Call of the Wild.* Man even resembles the beasts, assuming their physical features, their instinctual behavior. "What with the Fear of the North, the mental strain, and the ravages of the disease," wrote London in "In a Far Country," "they lost all semblance of humanity, taking on the appearance of wild beasts, hunted and desperate."[19] Both Buck and White Fang are men dressed in furs. When they brutally maim and devour opponents, London means humans, releasing complex hostilities in his makeup against the world, hostilities again traced to his birth and feelings of inferiority. Even Macmillan Company admitted this in *Jack London: His Life and Literary Works*: "In his two most important books, *The Call of the Wild*, and *White Fang*, he has reduced thought and emotion to their lowest terms. He has dared to treat animals like human beings—not symbolically, be it noted, but realistically and naturally—because he recognizes no essential difference between the so-called lower animals and man."[20] . . .

MISINFORMATION ON ANIMAL BEHAVIOR

London misinformed readers about animal behavior in *The Call of the Wild.* Buck, returning to the spoils of a kill, finds a dozen wolverines, among nature's most vicious creatures. "He scattered them like chaff; and those that fled left two behind who would quarrel no more."[21] (London used *wolves* and *wolverines* interchangeably in his stories, not realizing

17. Jack London, "The Somnambulists," *Independent*, 61 (July–December 1906), pp. 1451–54. 18. Don M. Wolfe, ed., *The Image of Man in America* (New York: Thomas Y. Crowell, 1970), pp. 203–4. 19. Jack London, *Son of the Wolf*, p. 92. 20. Brochure, *Jack London: His Life and Literary Works*, Macmillan Co. Courtesy of the I. Milo Shepard Estate. 21. Jack London, *The Call of the Wild*, p. 207.

that vicious wolverines would have slaughtered White Fang.) Buck also beats an entire wolf pack. . . . As Theodore Roosevelt reasoned: "The modern 'nature faker' is of course an object of derision to every scientist worthy of the name, to every real lover of the wilderness, to every faunal naturalist, to every true hunter or nature lover. But it is evident that he completely deceives many good people who are wholly ignorant of wild life. Sometimes he draws on his own imagination for his fictions; sometimes he gets them second-hand from irresponsible guides or trappers or Indians." [22]

The wolf remains Jack London's most outrageous deception, an animal he associated with cunning, fierce strength, and legendary inheritance traced to Romulus and Remus. "In spite of our sober biological outlook," writes Barry Lopez, "we can't seem to escape our fear of . . . [the wolf] hunter, any more than we can deny a fondness for the . . . [animal] because he seems to represent valued things that are slipping away from us—courage, wildness, self-sufficiency. Our fascination with the wolf may be rooted in a perception of him as the symbol of an internal war, the conflict between rational and instinctual behavior. This is the wolf of Aesopian fable." [23] Lopez adds in *Of Wolves and Men* that "London's novels show a preoccupation with 'the brute nature' in men, which he symbolized in the wolf. . . . But it is, ultimately, a neurotic fixation with machismo that has as little to do with wolves as the drinking, whoring, and fighting side of man's brute nature." [24] . . .

HUMANS TERRIFY WOLVES

Millions of Americans swallowed London's cruel fantasies as truth, not realizing human beings terrify wolves. "In North America, no scientifically acceptable evidence is available to support the claim that healthy wild wolves are dangerous to man," writes L. David Mech in *The Wolf.* "Even stronger evidence that healthy North American wolves are harmless to humans can be found in the many well-documented accounts of various researchers who have worked in wolf country. . . . In my own experiences with wolves I have never come close to danger." [25]

22. Theodore Roosevelt, "Nature Fakirs," *Everybody's Magazine*, 17 (July–December 1907), p. 428. 23. Barry Lopez, "What Are Wolves? Undoing the Myths," *Travel & Leisure*, 7 (January 1977), p. 7. 24. Barry Lolstun Lopez, *Of Wolves and Men* (New York: Scribners, 1978), p. 218. 25. L. David Mech, *The Wolf* (Garden City: Natural History Press, 1970), pp. 291, 292, 293.

Farley Mowat tells this story in *Never Cry Wolf*: "Quite by accident I had pitched my tent within ten yards of one of the major paths used by the wolves when they were going to, or coming from, their hunting grounds to the westward; and only a few hours after I had taken up residence one of the wolves came back from a trip and discovered me and my tent. . . . It was true that I wanted to be inconspicuous, but I felt uncomfortable at being so totally ignored. Nevertheless, during the two weeks which followed, one or more wolves used the track past my tent almost every night—and never, except on one memorable occasion, did they evince the slightest interest in me." [26]

Naturalist-cinematographer Bill Mason, who filmed "Cry of the Wild" for the Canadian Wildlife Services, writes me: "My captive wolves were terrified of me, despite all my efforts to befriend them. Only pups taken from the mother before two weeks old could be tamed and raised to accept the presence of humans without fear. If there is one single thing that I learned from all my experiences with wolves, it's that I would stake unequivocally that wolves are terrified of people. In fact I staked my life on it by travelling unarmed among them and alone. The only dangers I faced were from the extreme cold." [27]

Perhaps Roger A. Caras (author of *The Custer Wolf*, ABC-TV news correspondent and former vice-president of The Humane Society of the United States) makes the most penetrating remark about London and wolves, writing me that London was "an incurable romantic whose truth was instantly made and served up as needed. . . . He was not an authority on wolves, dogs, people, places or truth. He wrote and they bought it so he wrote some more." [28] Caras comments about London's Yukon stories: "He certainly was also devoted to the macho image. I have been around sled dogs (I cared for a championship team) and I have been in the Arctic and in Eskimo villages. It is rather more peaceful than super jock Jack London portrays." [29]

An obsession with wolves haunted London's life, another expression of his pathological involvement with symbols of fear and violence. As Sidney Alexander says, "The trouble

26. Farley Mowat, *Never Cry Wolf* (Boston: Little, Brown and Co., 1963), pp. 80–81. 27. Bill Mason to John Perry, February 5, 1977. 28. Roger A. Caras to John Perry, September 22, 1976, in *The Custer Wolf* (Boston: Little, Brown and Co., 1966). 29. Roger A. Caras to John Perry, May 14, 1978.

with Jack London was that he wasn't sure whether he was a man or a wolf."[30]. . . London had a wolf's head on his engraved stationery and bookmarks, signed his letters "Wolf," and named his sprawling ranch at Glen Ellen "Wolf House." [His friend] George Sterling called him "Wolf,"—something he asked [his second wife] Charmian to do more often. "In all his writings Jack London is changing dogs into wolves and wolves into dogs," remarked Stephen Graham. "In the course of it all London himself became a civilized dog, reconciled to kennel and master. But he constantly bays at men and the moon to assure them that he is wolf at heart."[31]

30. Sidney Alexander, "Jack London's Literary Lycanthropy," *Reporter*, 16 (January–June 1957), p. 46. 31. Stephen Graham, *The Death of Yesterday* (London: Ernest Benn, 1930), p. 58.

CHAPTER 2

Themes in *The Call of the Wild*

READINGS ON
THE CALL OF THE WILD

The Call of the Wild Is an Indictment of Humanity

Kate Blackiston Stillé

London's thrilling book uses the metaphor of a dog to reveal the savagery in all people and men's instinctive need to kill, writes Kate Blackiston Stillé in this 1903 review of *The Call of the Wild*. In the transformation of Buck, the dog, she sees the "going down of the true man, this awakening of the primeval man." Stillé finds in the book an indictment of the turn-of-the-century trend to savagery she identifies even among society girls, and calls for a change in attitude that would teach men rather than beat them.

A clear, strong picture of the battlefield of life with the colors laid on in a way that brings to the strong and thoughtful the consciousness of the spiritual and material conflict that rages between civilization and savagery. A dog, not a man, is the hero of the story which is less fiction than a serious problem, that reaches down into the heart of life, with an anguish that throbs and cries aloud on every page. Buck, the master-spirit, is a dog, well-born and well-bred; all that is interesting in the men comes out through their intercourse with this splendid dog. A cross between the St. Bernard and the Shepherd, gives the size, the endurance, the placidity, the intelligence, the gentleness and faithfulness that count in civilization and in the struggles of life.

THE SAVAGE WITHIN US

The Call of the Wild is the heart laid bare in that forcible, thrilling way that makes one groan in desperate resistance to the savage that is not worlds away, nor in ancestors dead and buried centuries ago, but within us. The truths of life under the

Reprinted from Kate Blackiston Stillé, Review of *The Call of the Wild*, from *Book News Monthly* 22, September 1903.

skillful handling of Jack London take possession and press themselves into the soul in such a way that we seem in the horrors of a nightmare powerless to resist, unnerved and helpless under "the law of club and fang." All phases of life are touched with the unerring skill of the true artist.

The brush brings out softly the sensuous captivating life in Southern California.

Civilization is both beautiful and capable, is at home on Judge Miller's place. Buck is "neither house-dog nor kennel-dog. The whole realm was his," but he was saved from being the pampered house-dog by hunting and outdoor sports, which the author cleverly shows is the type of the country gentleman who is ease-taking and at the same time has the careful oversight of the details which makes his estate great. Buck was kidnapped and sold into the Klondyke by the gardener's helper, whose character and needs are graphically told in that he was a gambler, had faith in it, "which made his damnation certain." He required money for his sin, and "the wages of the gardener's helper do not lap-over the needs of a wife and numerous progeny." The result of the passion and the necessity bring to us such suffering on the part of the dog, and such brutality from men that we comprehend as never before, that there is a devil in man and that the savage is not on the frontier, but at our door.

SHEDDING THE HANDICAP OF A MORAL NATURE

Buck knew not fear until he was beaten; he was of gentle blood and understood that he stood no chance against the man with the club, but his splendid lineage saved him from cowardice and stood the test of starvation and merciless toil. He was put to work to draw sledges, subjected to cruelty and toil, but when he learned "the law of club and fang" he won the leadership of the team. We see the passiveness drop and watch until the toil of the traces becomes the best expression of life. Then comes the transformation, necessitated by the ruthless struggle for existence. How swift and terrible the going to pieces of the moral nature, which is a vain thing and a heavy handicap under strenuous circumstances. This is the primitive code for man and beast—not to rob openly, but cunningly, "out of respect for club and fang," not to steal for joy; "but because of the clamor of an empty stomach."

This going down of the true man, this awakening of the primeval man, is desperately real. Sight and sense grow keen,

instincts long dead are alive, the savage nature is quickened, and the old tricks come back without effort. Buck came to his own again "when on the still cold nights he pointed his nose at a star and howled long and wolf-like, it was his ancestors, dead and dust, pointing nose at star and howling down through the centuries and through him. And his cadences were their cadences, and the cadences, which voiced their woe, and what to them was the meaning of the stillness and the cold and dark."

Through starvation and abuse Buck grew responsive to the call of the wild, and this he obeyed when Thornton, his only friend, was killed by the Indians.

Through the "comprehensive relation of things" Jack London shows that the heights and depths of the universe are within the soul, and no one has put it with such force and feeling, though all have known it.

How splendidly civilization brings out the fine steely strength that endures and triumphs; and how squarely the conditions of life are met. The thriftless, complaining go down! The strong and brutal overcome.

DEEP UNDERLYING TRUTH

The telling thing in the book is its deep underlying truth. The call of the wild is no fiction. The things pointed out are the nameless things we feel, and the author shows clearly, unobtrusively that it is "the old instincts which at stated periods drive men out from the sounding cities to forest and plain to kill things." That man and dog alike are mastered by the wolf-cry, striving after things alive, as it flees before them. Both sounding the deeps of his nature and of the parts of his nature that were deeper than he, "going back into the womb of Time."

The *Call of the Wild* penetrates to the very marrow and flows in the blood of the veins. Its manifestations are everywhere.

When the society girl "camps out for fun" and tyrannizes over and neglects her pets, ignores and treats the old with scant courtesy, she as surely obeys "the law of the club and fang" as Buck, when he relentlessly pursued the "foe he had started on the way to death."

This is true of soldiers, of university men, who enter mining camps and take to ranching, of men who leave their wives and firesides to sleep on the bare ground, of the nation's Chief, whose delight is in pursuing and killing big game, and who devotes the Cabinet room to sport, filling it with boxing gloves, swords and foils.

These may all be taken as the legitimate guides to the trend of the times, which muzzles and massacres the individual, that touches society with decay, and drags men back to the primeval forest where their hairy ancestors clung with long arms to the trees.

TRUE LEADERSHIP IS IN HUMANITY

The unknown self stands out on the pages of this thrilling romance, and from the depths of his heart the author says, Behold, you are no better than the—

New caught peoples,
    Half devil, half child.

To bring us to our waking life, more literature like *The Call of the Wild* is needed, and more men like Herbert Welsh, these the benefactors of humanity, teach us to lift men rather than club them. True leadership always is in humanity, and it is not enough to possess pity and mercy, but we must be possessed by them. These give real authority and go to the heart, moves and persuades it, though this is not the language of greed and blood, but that of the Divine will.

There is sublime and pathetic beauty in the way the brute comes out in this noble dog. Driven to his own by man's cruelty and yet triumphing over the brute, becoming the master and leader of the pack, outdoing them in cunning, defying the bravest hunter, like man, and yet unlike him, always surrounded with mystery, through the touch of the human. Alone every year the dog goes down to the spot where his master was killed, and with one long mournful howl, stands motionless as a statue, the wolfish nature dead before the unforgettable Love that drew him there.

In this little drama we are brought face to face with that which we refuse to confess to ourselves, and are chilled by the realism of *The Call of the Wild*, and bidden by it to listen to the Voice of the Divine, which also is a part of our being.

The Call of the Wild Is a Man's Book

Anonymous

The Call of the Wild is "real" literature, not make-believe, asserts the anonymous reviewer in this 1903 review. Though it should not be read by those looking for sentiment or love, anyone looking for a man's book of adventure about a great dog, as well as a true look at the brutal life of men and beasts in the harsh Northland, will not only enjoy the tale but want to read it again.

When Jack London, four years ago, wrote the stories that were gathered in *The Son of the Wolf*, all the critics recognized in him a master of the life of the Arctic, as all, a decade before, had acclaimed Kipling the master of the older and more complex life in India. There was no question of London's intimate first-hand knowledge of the trail under the midnight sun and of the fierce lust for gold that arouses in the miner the passions of the cave man of the stone age. This knowledge was stamped on every line. With it was joined a marvelous story-telling faculty that gripped the reader's interest and never let go until the end was reached. With it, too, went a purely pagan joy in living and fighting, and overcoming the obstacles that nature in the Far North throws in the way of man. Stripped of all sentimentality, these stories lay hold upon one like the tales told by one who comes out from the very presence of dreadful death and in whose eyes yet linger the glow of superb courage. Other stories Jack London has told in the meanwhile, but he has never reached the height of those first tales until he produced *The Call of the Wild*, which the Macmillan Company of New York bring out now in fine style, with a number of illustrations by Philip R. Goodwin and Charles Livingston Bull. It is the story of a dog's life in the Far North, but this record of a splendid ca-

Reprinted from an anonymous review of *The Call of the Wild*, in *The San Francisco Chronicle*, August 2, 1903.

nine hero is really a marvelously graphic picture of the great gold rush to the Klondike in 1897, and of the life of the packer and the miner in Alaska. Compared with this all other stories or sketches of this second great gold rush of the nineteenth century pale into insignificance. Fierce, brutal, splashed with blood, and alive with the crack of whip and blow of club, it is yet a story that sounds the deep note of tenderness between man and beast, and that loyalty and fidelity which never falters even in the jaws of death. And beyond all this is the strange haunting charm of "the call of the wild" to the savage strain in the big dog, arousing dormant instincts that have come down to him from his wolf ancestors. At times this is pushed perilously far, but in nothing has Jack London shown more clearly his artistic mastery than in making real to the reader the hereditary instincts that the savage life of the north brings out in the great dog, the hero of this story. Once only is a false note struck, and that is at the end, when he makes the dog return every year to mourn over the grave of the master whom he loved.

A THRILLING STORY

Buck, the hero, is a huge animal, a cross between a St. Bernard and a Scotch shepherd. He is stolen from his comfortable home in the Santa Clara valley and sold to a man, who takes him to Seattle. There he passes into the hands of a professional dealer in dogs, who makes him understand the power of a club wielded by a skillful hand. Then he is sold at a high price as a dog fit to draw a sledge over the frozen snow and ice from Skagway to Dawson. And now begins a really thrilling story of the training of this dog in the mastery of the trail, until he becomes not only the champion fighter of the Klondike, but the finest sledge dog in the Arctic. Very skillfully London develops the advantages which his good blood brings him. He is early taught what the author calls "the law of club and fang." He learns that this life and death struggle on the trail admits of no sentiment and no honors; that mercy enters not into it, nor kindness. He learns that dogs and men respect only the supremacy of brute force and cunning, and that justice is dealt out with unsparing hand. He quickly learns all that is to be taught of the lore of the trail, but his ambition rises to be master of the team on which he works. Before many weeks he has had his first great fight for supremacy with the old leader of the team. He conquers, and the old dog goes down to death under his savage fangs. He has several owners, mostly half-breeds, who carry the mail and official dispatches from tide water to Dawson. These men are drawn with only a few strokes, but each one stands out clear and recognizable, even to his mongrel French-English. Then, when Buck and the other dogs are worn to the bone with the fatigue of forced marches, they are sold by the Government to a tenderfoot party. From the handling of masters of the trail they pass to the cruelty of incompetents. Nothing in the book is better done than the short episode of the two men and one woman, who start for the land of gold with no training and no qualities of strength, patience and endurance that would make them able to cope with cold, fatigue and hardship. At White River the dogs drop in their traces and the brutal driver is beating Buck to death, when John Thornton, a prospector, interferes and saves the dog's life. The tenderfoot gang, in the face of warnings, press on and soon go down to death in the river through a hole in the rotten ice.

Then begins a new life for Buck. His master is slowly recovering from the effects of frozen feet and is waiting for his partners to return in the spring. Thornton learns to love the dog and he is repaid with a devotion that is sometimes startling. Twice the huge dog saves the life of the man who befriended him, and once he wins for him a large sum by putting forth his enormous strength. Finally Thornton and his partners strike rich ground in a remote section. There they stay many weeks. In his ample leisure Buck haunts the woods, and the visions of the old days when he roamed the forests as a wolf come back to him with renewed strength. But when he meets a wolf far in the woods and they fraternize, he cannot bring himself to abandon the man whom he loves. One day the instinct to hunt and kill comes over him when he espies a big bull moose. He follows the herd for hours, cuts out the bull, and, after two days, wears down its strength and kills it. On his return he finds that a band of Indians have attacked the mining camp and slain the prospectors. With a roar of rage and grief Buck suddenly leaps upon them, tearing at the men's throats, and so fierce is his attack and so fearful the wounds that he inflicts that the whole band is routed. Then, having avenged in some sort his master's murder, he turns to the woods and joins the band of wolves. Thus he succumbs at last to "the call of the wild."

POWERFUL DRAMA

Many passages were marked in the reading of this book, but most are too long for quotation. Good examples of fine dramatic power are the description of the breaking in of Buck at Seattle, the fight for the mastery of the team with Spitz, the winning of Thornton's wager and the trailing of the old moose. Some of the finest descriptive passages, cast in prose but full of poetic charm, are those which deal with the dog's harking back to his primordial days when he ranged over the north with the cave men. Here is a specimen of these visions which the dog dreamed by the campfire:

> The Sunland was very dim and distant, and such memories had no power over him. Far more potent were the memories of his heredity that gave things he had never seen before a seeming familiarity; the instincts (which were but the memories of his ancestors become habits), which had lapsed in later days, and still later, in him, quickened and become alive again. Sometimes, as he crouched there, blinking dreamily at the flames, it seemed that the flames were of another fire, and that as he crouched by this other fire he saw another and different man from the half-breed cook before him. This other man was shorter of leg and longer of arm, with muscles that were stringy and knotty, rather than rounded and swelling. The hair of this man was long and matted, and his head slanted back under it from the eyes. He uttered strange sounds, and seemed very much afraid of the darkness, into which he peered continually.

> At other times this hairy man squatted by the fire with head between his legs and slept. On such occasions his elbows were on his knees, his hands clasped above his head, as though to shed rain by the hairy arms. And beyond that fire, in the circling darkness, Buck could see many gleaming coals, two by two, always two by two, which he knew to be the eyes of great beasts of prey. And he could hear the crashing of their bodies through the undergrowth, and the noises they made in the night. And dreaming there by the Yukon bank, with lazy eyes blinking at the fire, these sights and sounds of another world would make the hair to rise along his back and to stand on end across his shoulders and up his neck, till he whimpered low and suppressedly or growled softly, and the half-breed cook shouted at him. "Hey, you, Buck, wake up!" Whereupon the other world would vanish and the real world come into his eyes, and he would get up and yawn and stretch as though he had been asleep.

There is space here for only one more extract, which is a powerful reiteration of the law of the survival of the fittest:

> His face and body were scarred by the teeth of many dogs and he fought as fiercely as ever and more shrewdly. And Buck

was merciless. He had learned well the law of club and fang, and he never forewent an advantage or drew back from a foe he had started on the way to death. He had lessoned from Spitz and from the chief fighting dogs of the police and mail, and knew there was no middle course. He must master or be mastered; while to show mercy was a weakness. Mercy did not exist in the primordial life. It was misunderstood for fear, and such misunderstandings made for death. Kill or be killed, eat or be eaten, was the law, and this mandate, down out of the depths of time, he obeyed.

And equally true with this is the pride of the sledge dog in his efficiency. Buck illustrates this when he claims the leader's position after he had killed Spitz, and Dave, the old wheel dog, also illustrates it very pathetically in his terrible efforts to keep up with the team and in his despair when he can no longer pull in the traces. It would be idle to recommend this book to any one who wishes love or sentiment. It is a man's book, through and through, but any one fond of dogs or of life and adventure in the Far North will be glad to read the book, and to read it more than once. In nothing else that Jack London has written has he shown so clearly as in this his complete mastery of his material and that unconscious molding of style to thought which marks real from make-believe literature.

Restoring Buck to the Role of a King

Joan D. Hedrick

The domestication of Buck created an artificial separation between the animal and his true nature, declares Joan D. Hedrick. The book describes the mythic restoration of a king as he is initiated into his rightful estate. Hedrick, author of *Solitary Comrade: Jack London and His Work*, from which this viewpoint is excerpted, has also published a biography of Harriet Beecher Stowe.

The Call of the Wild is a lyric not to what is possible or logical but to what the heart desires. . . .

Like *The Sea-Wolf* and many another naturalistic tale, it begins with the abrupt transportation of a sheltered upper-class hero "into the primitive." At Judge Miller's estate in the Santa Clara valley, Buck is the favorite dog. Referring to the judge's buildings and grounds, London writes "over this great demesne Buck ruled" (*CW*, 17).[1] It is his privilege to accompany the judge and his sons and daughters and grandchildren wherever they go, and Buck "stalked imperiously" before the other dogs, "for he was king,—king over all creeping, crawling, flying things of Judge Miller's place, humans included" (*CW*, 18). When gold is discovered in the Klondike, a premium is put on dogs like Buck, who are strong and have warm furry coats. One night when the judge is away, Manuel, an underpaid gardener, steals Buck and sells him to cover his gambling debts. Here begins Buck's education as to his true estate. When a rope is put around his neck, he accepts it with "quiet dignity," still trusting in the wisdom of human masters. But when the end of the rope is handed to a stranger, Buck "growls menacingly," believing that "to intimate was to com-

1. Jack London, *The Call of the Wild*. New York: Grosset & Dunlap, 1915. Subsequent page references are to this edition.

Adapted from *Solitary Comrade: Jack London and His Work* by Joan D. Hedrick. Copyright © 1982 by the University of North Carolina Press. Used by permission of the publisher.

mand" (*CW*, 20). Instead of hearkening to his royal wishes, this stranger tightens the rope around his neck. When Buck springs at the man, the rope tightens and Buck is helpless—and enraged. "Never in all his life had he been so vilely treated, and never in all his life had he been so angry" (*CW*, 21). Buck's anger waxes as, instead of being released, he is put into a cage, tormented through the bars by his keepers, and finally put on an express car. After having changed hands many times, Buck meets the man in the red sweater who is the dog-breaker. Against this man is unleashed the mighty anger that has waxed in the heart of this "kidnapped king." "Straight at the man he launched his one hundred and forty pounds of fury, surcharged with the pent passion of two days and nights." But in mid-air, Buck's hurling body is stopped by the blow of a club. "He had never been struck by a club in his life, and did not understand." Again and again he launches himself against this man, for "his madness knew no caution." But each time "the club broke the charge and smashed him down" (*CW*, 28). The man in the red sweater finishes him off with a blow directly on his nose, and a final "shrewd blow" knocks him unconscious. As an onlooker comments, this man is "no slouch at dog-breakin'." The man later brings Buck water and food, and Buck allows him to touch him and even eats from his hand.

London is clear about the effect of this experience on Buck. "He was beaten (he knew that); but he was not broken. He saw, once for all, that he stood no chance against a man with a club. He had learned the lesson, and in all his after life he never forgot it. That club was a revelation" (*CW*, 30). The lesson is reinforced as Buck watches other dogs being initiated. "Again and again, as he looked at each brutal performance, the lesson was driven home to Buck: a man with a club was a law-giver, a master to be obeyed, though not necessarily conciliated. Of this last Buck was never guilty, though he did see beaten dogs that fawned upon the man, and wagged their tails, and licked his hand. Also he saw one dog, that would neither conciliate nor obey, finally killed in the struggle for mastery" (*CW*, 31). This initiation serves Buck well in the Northland, where he must take on a new psychology—the psychology of a dependent people—if he is to survive. When the "kidnapped king" is put in harness, "his dignity was sorely hurt by thus being made a draught animal, [but] he was too wise to rebel" (*CW*, 42). He has not forgotten his kingly heritage, but he cunningly hides his desire for mastery, "bid[ing] his time with a patience that was nothing less than primitive" (*CW*, 74). . . .

RESTORATION TO HERITAGE AND TRADITION

The Call of the Wild is the story of an animal who, having been domesticated, was artificially removed from his rightful culture and traditions, and who is, in the story, restored to that heritage. The first step in that process is the initiation, which reveals to him his true state. Then gradually Buck is restored to the older tradition from which he had been cut off. . . .

Buck's restoration to his rightful kingdom proceeds in four stages, which are characterized by the contrasting masters under whom he works. Perrault and François, the government couriers under whom Buck first works, are just and efficient masters. The taciturn Perrault, chosen for his job because "nothing daunted him," labors grimly from dawn to dark, his consciousness focused only on the job of delivering the despatches as speedily as possible. His garrulous companion, François, is endowed with a bit more imagination and humor than Perrault, but he is just as concentrated on the job at hand. Both are expert managers of their dogs, upon whose energy and cooperation depends the task of delivering the mail. François's impartial administration of justice keeps peace among the huskies and wins Buck's respect. Although Buck accepts the rule of François and Perrault, he challenges the authority of Spitz, whose role as lead dog is analogous to that of a foreman on a line. Spitz keeps discipline among the dogs. The order and efficiency of the team is disrupted by Buck's challenge to his authority, which sends a mutinous ripple throughout the ranks. François understands that the competition between the dogs will eventually end in a fight to the death, but he does not see all the petty insubordinations with which Buck cunningly lays down his challenge to Spitz. Buck, the onetime pet of the upper class, is now like a blond beast, riding high within a system in which the strong eat the weak. After Buck has fought Spitz to the death, the other dogs, who have been hungrily waiting, close in to feast on the victim. "Buck stood and looked on, the successful champion, the dominant primordial beast who had made his kill and found it good" (*CW*, 89).

Buck's desire for mastery is now spent upon his fellow dogs. In a later stage of his restoration he will question the authority of his human masters, but even in this first stage Buck's consciousness is more developed than that of most of his teammates. This may be seen in the contrast between Buck and two of the most experienced and knowledgeable dogs, Dave and Sol-leks. The joy of work is strong in all of the sled dogs, but in Dave and Sol-leks, it is a passionate pride. Apathetic under most circumstances, they are reborn when put in the traces. . . . The petty fights that break out among the other dogs do not interest Dave and Sol-leks. Nor do they seek advancement through the ranks. After Buck has killed Spitz, François harnesses Sol-leks, whom he judges to be "the best lead-dog left," in the coveted position. When Buck asserts his prerogatives and springs upon Sol-leks, the old dog is only too eager to give over the position to Buck, of whom he is afraid (*CW*, 94). Although the endurance and pride of dogs like Dave and Sol-leks are admirable, they do not have the imagination of Buck, who is able to see beyond the toil of the traces to a larger game. Dave and Sol-leks are, for all their pride, destined to be work-beasts.

FROM BAD TO WORSE

The importance of Buck's larger vision becomes evident in the next interlude; François and Perrault depart, and a "Scotch half-breed" takes charge of the team, which becomes part of a large mail train en route to Dawson. The drivers are considerate of their dogs and do what they can for them, but conditions are against men and dogs. The dogs are exhausted from their earlier runs and should have had a week's rest before starting out again. The mail is heavy, and daily snowfalls increase the friction on the runners. The dogs' pride in their work remains, but competing for attention in London's descriptions are details that suggest the industrial routine in which they labor: "Buck did not like it, but he bore up well to the work, taking pride in it after the manner of Dave and Sol-leks, and seeing that his mates, whether they prided in it or not, did their fair share. It was a monotonous life, operating with machine-like regularity. One day was very like another" (*CW*, 100–101). Buck challenges three other dogs and wins leadership of the team, but this fact goes almost unnoticed, so lacking in drama is it after the elaborately prepared-for battle with Spitz. The glamour of being a "blond beast" is subtly undermined by a vision of the limits of this route to mastery. The chapter ends, significantly, with the death of Dave. . . .

Buck's third set of masters may be dispensed with quickly. The dogs are not allowed to recover their now seriously flagging energies before they are sold to three incompetents from the States, who are, interestingly, "a nice family party"—a husband and wife and the wife's younger brother—rather than a work team. They quarrel, they overload the sled, they get late starts every morning, and worse, they miscalculate the amount of food they must carry for the dogs. The dogs begin to die, one by one, and the remaining team and drivers are finally swallowed up when the men insist on crossing the ice during the spring thaw. Buck is saved from this end by his refusal to obey the command to cross the ice. He does not trust these masters, and, oppressed by a sense of impending calamity, he lies down in the traces and refuses to budge, even though he is whipped repeatedly. He was prepared to die in this mutiny, but a man watching the beating forcefully intervenes. This man is John Thornton, destined to become Buck's last and most beloved master.

THE BONDS OF LOVE

Up to this point, Buck's situation has worsened with each change of masters. The limits that are placed on dogs by their dependency on human masters have been starkly dramatized in the last episode, in which the masters are not competent enough to look out for even their own best interests. It is at this point, when Buck might most logically have made a run for freedom and independence, that London introduces him to a master who is qualitatively different. The bonds that tied Perrault and François to Buck were bonds of duty and work and were lightly snapped. The bonds that tie Buck and John Thornton are bonds of love and can be broken, if at all, only by death. The chapter entitled "For the Love of a Man" treads a fine line between sentimentality and deep emotion; the balance comes down on the side of deep emotion, and one doubts that London could have achieved this were he writing about a father and his child rather than a man and his dog. "This man had saved his life, which was something; but, further, he was the ideal master. Other men saw to the welfare of their dogs from a sense of duty and business expediency; he saw to the welfare of his *as if they were his own children, because he could not help it*" (*CW*, 149; my emphasis). As Thornton saved Buck's life, Buck will later have the opportunity to save Thornton's life. The covenant thus forged between man and dog cannot be measured in ordinary terms, nor is Buck's trust of Thornton a calculated thing. When Thornton, in a moment of thoughtless whim, commands Buck to jump over a cliff, Buck responds instantly and unthinkingly, for he had already demonstrated that he would give his life for Thornton if he requested it. (Only Thornton's last-minute scramble to grab Buck at the edge of the cliff prevents his jumping.) Besides these heroic demonstrations of their bonding, Thornton and Buck have a language in which they communicate their affection from day to day. "Buck had a trick of love expression that was akin to hurt. He would often seize Thornton's hand in his mouth and close so fiercely that the flesh bore the impress of his teeth for some time afterward. And as Buck understood [John Thornton's] oaths to be love words, so the man understood this feigned bite for a caress" (*CW*, 150).

The emotional peak of their relationship occurs when Thornton—again rather thoughtlessly—asserts in front of others that Buck can break out a sled loaded with one thousand pounds of goods. Bets are placed. Buck is harnessed to a sled loaded with one thousand pounds of flour. Thornton does not know whether or not Buck can perform this extraordinary feat, but he grabs the dog's head and shakes it back and forth as was his affectionate habit and whispers to the dog, "As you love me, Buck. As you love me" (*CW*, 170). Buck does it for love.

> Thornton fell on his knees beside Buck. Head was against head, and he was shaking him back and forth. Those who hurried up heard him cursing Buck, and he cursed him long and fervently, and softly and lovingly.
>
> "Gad, sir! Gad, sir!" spluttered the Skookum Bench king. "I'll give you a thousand for him, sir, a thousand, sir—twelve hundred, sir."
>
> Thornton rose to his feet. His eyes were wet. The tears were streaming frankly down his cheeks. "Sir," he said to the Skookum Bench king, "no, sir. You can go to hell, sir. It's the best I can do for you, sir."
>
> Buck seized Thornton's hand in his teeth. Thornton shook him back and forth. As though animated by a common impulse, the onlookers drew back to a respectful distance; nor were they again indiscreet enough to interrupt. [*CW*, 172–73]

Buck has worked harder than he ever has before, and is, in his blind love of John Thornton, more dependent than he has ever been before. Yet this love dependency, this total giving up of self to another and total entrusting of his life to another is necessary before Buck can strike out on his own and be restored to the culture and traditions from which he has been separated. *The Call of the Wild* is set apart from all of London's other quest stories by the emotional satisfaction granted the hero (and the reader). This quest is different from the others, too, in that the hero seeks not a nurturant mother, who inevitably reveals her rapacious designs, but a father, who remains to the end the good father, who cares for his dogs "as if they were his own children, because he could not help it."

Having truly been a child, Buck is now prepared to grow up. More and more insistently he hears a call from the forest: "It filled him with a great unrest and strange desires. It caused him to feel a vague, sweet gladness, and he was aware of wild yearnings and stirrings for he knew not what. Sometimes he pursued the call into the forest, looking for it as though it were a tangible thing, barking softly or defiantly, as the mood might dictate" (*CW*, 183). . . . He begins to stay away from camp for longer and longer periods, "seeking vainly for fresh sign of the wild brother, killing his meat as he traveled" (*CW*, 190). Buck's hunting exploits are an important part of this interlude. "The blood-longing became stronger than ever before. He was a killer, a thing that preyed, living on the things that lived, unaided, alone, by virtue of his own strength and prowess, surviving triumphantly in a hostile environment where only the strong survived" (*CW*, 191).

THE TIE IS BROKEN

Through these exploits he develops "a great pride in himself which communicated itself like a contagion to his physical being" (*CW*, 191). Just before his apotheosis, Buck is pictured in the prime of his life: "His muscles were surcharged with vitality, and snapped into play sharply, like steel springs. Life streamed through him in splendid flood, glad and rampant, until it seemed that it would burst him asunder in sheer ecstasy and pour forth generously over the world" (*CW*, 193). In his desire for larger and larger prey, Buck runs down a great moose, having patiently trailed him for four days. After feasting on the moose, he turns back toward the camp, but as he goes, he is "oppressed with a sense of calamity" (*CW*, 200). When he reaches the camp, he finds it has been raided by the Yeehat Indians, who have left their victims riddled with arrows. Buck madly avenges himself on the Yeehats, and then returns to look for John Thornton. He follows his scent "down to the edge of a deep pool," which "effectually hid what it contained, and it contained John Thornton" (*CW*, 204). Buck broods by the side of the pool, feeling "a void which ached and ached, and which food could not fill." He also feels pride when he remembers that in avenging himself on the Yeehats, he has killed the noblest game of all—man. Most importantly, the death of John Thornton has freed Buck to follow the call from the place whence it came. "The last tie was broken. Man and the claims of man no longer bound him" (*CW*, 206).

Buck hears the call, "sounding more luringly and compelling than ever before." He meets the wolf pack in the clearing, and "they were awed, so still and large he stood" (*CW*, 207). Buck swiftly breaks the neck of the first wolf to challenge him and bloodies the three others who "tried it in sharp succession" (*CW*, 207). The whole pack joins in the challenge, and Buck holds them off for half an hour, when they fall back exhausted. At this point one wolf separates himself from the pack and approaches Buck, whining softly. Buck recognizes "the wild brother with whom he had run for a night and a day." They touch noses, and then an old wolf, patriarch of the tribe, comes over, also sniffs noses with Buck, and then points his nose at the sky and breaks into "the long wolf howl" (*CW*, 208). The tribal song is taken up by the whole pack, and Buck joins in. "Then, acting as one body, the pack sprang away into the woods. And Buck ran with them, side by side with the wild brother, yelping as he ran" (*CW*, 209).

Buck has been initiated into the tribe and restored to his rightful kingdom. No more does he submit himself to the rule of man. Whereas once he pursued his desire for mastery within an industrial order prescribed by human masters, he now runs by the side of his wood brother. His consciousness has undergone several revolutions: from his initial kingly pretensions, which hid from himself his actual dependency on Judge Miller's largesse, Buck came to realize his true position; his education proceeded dialectically as he first asserted his leadership over the dog pack and then totally submitted to John Thornton out of love. In his final apotheosis, Buck achieves the reconciliation of his desire for mastery and the desires aroused by the old call from the forest. His desire to be king is wedded to the radical egalitarianism implied by his relationship with his wood brother. In the last sentence of the tale, Buck leaps into our memories, serene and triumphant.

"When the long winter nights come on and the wolves follow their meat into the lower valleys, he may be seen running at the head of the pack through the pale moonlight or glimmering borealis, leaping gigantic above his fellows, his great throat a-bellow as he sings a song of the younger world, which is the song of the pack" (*CW*, 210–11). Buck's integration of himself is achieved by going back in time to a "younger world." The kidnapped king has been restored to his tribal community.

Like James Fenimore Cooper's hero, Leatherstocking, Buck moves from age to golden youth. His discovery of his wood brother, like the Deerslayer's pact with Chingachgook, puts him in touch with a natural community, and through this bond, he is immortalized. The body will die, but the consciousness that has been rooted in a community will live with that community and its traditions. In *The Call of the Wild* London resolves the terrible choice between self-advancement and solidarity in such a way that neither must be sacrificed. Buck is the canine equivalent of a street-gang leader, and *The Call of the Wild* is a mythic affirmation of the author's working-class origins, of a solidarity that is strength. But in order to make this affirmation, the story must be taken back into the "womb of time," into a tribal, precapitalistic world. The lyric intensity and beauty of this work arise from the deep satisfaction that author and reader experience at having the contradictions of our society mythically resolved.

Seven Stages of Allegory in *The Call of the Wild*

Michael Kumin

The Call of the Wild represents an allegory of the idyllic quest for self-actualization, writes Michael Kumin. The seven stages Buck must pass through, each marked by a significant event, finally lead to his elevation to a godlike rank. Kumin outlines the stages of this human allegory to explain why the novel should be considered a classic of both American and world literature.

Much of the popular success of *The Call of the Wild* was due to London's human allegory. . . . The main character [Buck] is a large canine, a character with whom most humans would be unable to find much similarity. Accepting the notion that most books are made popular by the popularity of their main character, and noting *The Call of the Wild*'s huge success with the public, we can assume that London's readers were, in different ways, able to identify with Buck. . . .

London's human allegory deals with the idyllic quest of everyone for self-actualization, the pursuit to be the best that you can possibly be. He traverses this complex subject by leading Buck through a series of seven stages. We are led to believe that only through this tiered process can animal, and allegorically, man, truly achieve apotheosis.[1] These seven steps each have a significant event attached to them, and it is this event that distinguishes when a stage begins or ends. In the first stage, our hero is born into society. This birth and innocence is peaceful, just as in infancy. The second stage begins and ends with the initiation into society. This event is often the turning point in the life of our hero. It marks the

1. Apotheosis: Elevation of a person to the rank of a god.

Reprinted from Michael Kumin, "*The Call of the Wild:* London's Seven Stages of Allegory," *Jack London Newsletter*, vol. 21, nos. 1–3, 1988.

first time that society's rules are imposed upon the free-thinking, free-acting innocence of youth. The third stage involves learning the laws and moral codes of society. Our hero must adapt to the society in which he lives, and learn to profit from its rules. The fourth stage begins when our hero has learned the laws of society, even mastered them, and now must bear the weight of that responsibility. After a period of time, after that weight has become tiresome and extreme, the fifth stage begins. The fifth stage is the symbolic death which our hero undergoes. Our hero is separated from the pretenders when he is able to emerge from this death and proceed to the sixth stage. The sixth stage is the symbolic rebirth which our hero undergoes after "death." It is here where our hero receives the energy and rejuvenation to enter the seventh and final stage. The seventh stage involves the apotheosis, or deification, which few will undergo. Our hero is strong enough to struggle through these seven stages to reach his final goal—self-actualization. It is through this seven-staged process that each and every animal proceeds. Few, if any, will reach the seventh and final stage. Buck, however, was one animal who traversed the difficult terrain and remained standing in the end. London uses this tiered process to paint a provoking human allegory through the use of his canine hero, Buck.

INNOCENCE

London begins the novel by describing Buck's peaceful upbringing. Living with the Judge in the Santa Clara Valley, Buck was free to do as he wished. London describes the peaceful setting where Buck roamed in the first chapter:

> But Buck was neither house-dog nor kennel dog. The whole realm was his. He plunged into the swimming tank or went hunting with the Judge's sons; he escorted Mollie and Alice, the Judge's daughters, on long twilight or early morning rambles; on wintry nights he lay at the Judge's feet before the roaring library fire; he carried the Judge's grandsons on his back, or rolled them in the grass, and guarded their footsteps through wild adventures down to the fountain in the stable yard, and even beyond, where the paddocks were, and the berry patches.

In this descriptive paragraph, London illustrates the serene, loving setting into which Buck was born. This peaceful background is similar to that of a young child's, in that both haven't a care in the world. Most people look back on their early years with fondness, and it is here that London begins to draw us towards Buck. London also sets up this "Garden of Eden" to later contrast it with the bleak "Hell" which Buck is drawn into. Early in the novel, London attempts to familiarize us with Buck, and let us grow fond of him.

London offers some foreshadowing immediately, as he begins his novel in a powerful fashion. Buck is portrayed as being helpless to forces which he cannot control:

> Buck did not read the newspapers, or he would have known that trouble was brewing, not alone for himself, but for every tidewater dog, strong of muscle and with warm, long hair, from Puget Sound to San Diego. Because men, groping in the Arctic darkness, had found a yellow metal, and because steamship and transportation companies were booming the find, thousands of men were rushing into the Northland. These men wanted dogs, and the dogs they wanted were heavy dogs, with strong muscles by which to toil, and furry coats to protect them from the frost.

In this opening paragraph, London describes the Gold Rush from a different point of view—that of the dogs. In the final sentence, London tells of foreboding "toil," an image which we will discuss later. London offers early foreshadowing in *The Call of the Wild* to brace the reader for Buck's short-lived life of serenity.

London uses the first stage of self-actualization, that of innocence, to help us identify with Buck. London opens his novel with a message of innocence, the fact that Buck was unaware of the Gold Rush, and thus unaware of his fate. Like a small child, Buck is helpless before this fate, and must depend on others for protection. We immediately identify with this helpless figure, and are angered when he is removed from this peaceful environment. This setting is the mother of Buck, the womb, if you will, from where he sprang. Since his parents are dead, we identify Buck's family to be that of Judge Miller's, and are thus upset when he is stolen away from this family. London uses the theme of innocence so that the reader will identify his character of Buck.

INITIATION INTO SOCIETY

Buck enters the second stage in his symbolic encounter with the man in the red sweater. After being sold off by the Judge's gardener, Buck is taken to the Northland. It is during this trip that he meets the man in the red sweater. The man's job was to break the spirit of the new dogs, and make them obey humans. This was no easy task with Buck, as he was reluctant to give up the peaceful ways of Judge Miller's home. After spending over two days and nights in a wooden crate without food or water, Buck was enraged and came to the point of violence. It is at this point that he is initiated into the society of the Northland:

> Straight at the man he launched his one hundred and forty pounds of fury, surcharged with the pent passion of two days and nights. In mid air, just as his jaws were about to close on the man, he received a shock that checked his body and brought his teeth together with a agonizing clip. He whirled over, fetching the ground on his back and side. He had never been struck by a club in his life, and did not understand. With a snarl that was part bark and more scream he was again on his feet and launched into the air. And again the shock came and he was brought crushingly to the ground. This time he was aware that it was the club, but his madness knew no caution. A dozen times he charged, and as often the club broke the charge and smashed him down.

In this powerful scene, Buck is introduced to the society in which he is to spend the rest of his life. As would be expected, he resists this change, but in the end, he comes to accept it. People identify with this scene by remembering the first time that they were forced to obey the laws of society, whether it be the first day of school or any similar instance. In all cases, we are forced to subdue our personal impulses in order to function within our society. This can be a painful lesson as we see in the case of Buck.

London furthers the human allegory by attributing human characteristics to Buck. In the previous passage, Buck exhibits a "snarl that was part bark and more scream." This phrase suggests that Buck had a more human than canine response. This would be simply a use of personification if the incident were isolated. However, if we look at the novel from a comprehensive perspective, it is clear that this is another example of London's human allegory.

Buck's initiation into society ends with the acceptance and realization of his role. Back at Judge Miller's home, Buck was free to do as he pleased. However, in the world of the Northland, Buck realizes that the club is law, and the man who wields it is God:

> He was beaten (he knew that); but he was not broken. He saw, once for all, that he stood no chance against a man with a club. He had learned the lesson, and in all his after life he

never forgot it. That club was a revelation. It was his introduction to the reign of primitive law, and he met the introduction halfway. . . . The lesson was driven home to Buck: a
man with a club was a law-giver, a master to be obeyed,
though not necessarily conciliated.

In this passage, Buck comes to the realization that, to live
in his new society, he must abide by the rules of its people.
He may not necessarily like those rules, but must come to
accept them. It is this acceptance that signifies the end of the
second stage, and beginning of the third.

LEARNING THE LAWS AND CODES

It is in the third stage that Buck learns the "Law of Club and
Fang." Buck learns early in the Northland to trust no one. He
is fortunate that his lesson is a vicarious one, "else he would
not have lived to profit by it". The incident involved Curly,
the good-natured Newfoundland who was Buck's first acquaintance in the Northland.

They were camped near the log store, where she, in her
friendly way, made advances to a husky dog the size of a full-
grown wolf, though not half so large as she. There was no
warning, only a leap in like a flash, a metallic clip of teeth, a
leap out equally swift, and Curly's face was ripped open from
eye to jaw.

It is in this scene that Buck learns of this foreign manner
of fighting. However, there was much more to the law of club
and fang.

It was the wolf manner of fighting, to strike and leap away;
but there was more to it than this. Thirty or forty huskies ran
to the spot and surrounded the combatants in an intent and
silent circle.

After the husky was able to knock Curly off her feet, the
mob of dogs closed in on her, leaving her mutilated body in
shreds. Buck sees the violence that exists in his new society.
He begins to fully comprehend the law of club and fang. "So
that was the way. No fair play. Once down, that was the end
of you. Well, he would see to it that he never went down".
Buck has learned his first rule of society, and is likely never
to forget it. It is with this bloody introduction that Buck begins the third stage.

As time passes, and Buck spends more time in his new society, he begins to understand, even master the law of club
and fang. Buck learns the rules of his new environment
quickly, easily forgetting the laws of his former life. Earle

Labor seems to agree with this assertion in his book, *Jack London*: "But more significant is the metamorphosis of his moral values. He learns, for example, that stealing, an unthinkable misdeed in his former state, can be the difference between survival and death". The event that Labor is referring to occurs when Buck, after carefully observing the methods of other dogs, steals an entire chunk of bacon from his dog-sled owner. What makes the event even more satisfying to Buck is that he goes unsuspected, whereas another dog is punished for the theft. London describes the changes that Buck has undergone since his arrival in the Northland:

> This first theft marked Buck as fit to survive in the hostile Northland environment. It marked his adaptability, his capacity to adjust himself to changing conditions, the lack of which would have meant swift and terrible death. It marked, further, the decay or going to pieces of his moral nature, a vain thing and a handicap in the ruthless struggle for existence.

Buck clearly adapts quickly to his newfound surroundings. London further illustrates his point in the following paragraph:

> All his days, no matter what the odds, he had never run from a fight. But the club of the man in the red sweater had beaten into him a more fundamental and primitive code. Civilized, he could have died for a moral consideration, say the defence of Judge Miller's riding whip; but the completeness of his decivilization was now evidenced by his ability to flee from the defence of a moral consideration and so save his hide. He did not steal for joy of it, but because of the clamor of his stomach. He did not rob openly, but stole secretly and cunningly, out of respect for club and fang.

We see that in these two passages, Buck has not only learned the law of club and fang, but learned how to prosper in it. He has forsaken his culture from the past, and has educated himself in the laws of his new society. He has emerged from being one of the many students of his culture, to shine as one of its most adept pupils. Just as humans undergo the maturation process, so does Buck learn the laws of his newfound home. London's allegorical meaning during Buck's third stage is clear. Humans learn the laws of society until they have been mastered. It is at this point that they bear the responsibilities of their mastery. Buck is similar in that he must also bear the burden of his knowledge. London illustrates Buck's dramatic changes in the third stage of development.

THE WEIGHT OF RESPONSIBILITY

After mastering the law of club and fang, Buck rises above all others to become the ideal dog in his society. Not only does Buck adjust to the law of club and fang, he becomes the leader of a group he once found barbaric and vile. Thus, his symbolic metamorphosis is complete; after he has learned all that society can offer him, his education is finished. When he has become the model for other dogs, it is clear that he has mastered the system. It is then that Buck enters the fourth stage, where he must bear the weight of his knowledge.

As Buck enters the fourth stage, we see a dog well-versed in the rules of society, ready to toil in the trenches of the dog sled. This period of Buck's life occurs while pulling for Perrault and Francois, and also for the Scotch half-breed and the mail-train drivers. This is a period of great pride in the life of Buck, but also one of wear and tear. Buck exhibits his mastery of the trail immediately after he assumed leadership:

> At a bound Buck took up the duties of leadership; and where judgment was required, and quick thinking and quick acting, he showed himself the superior even to Spitz, of whom Francois had never seen an equal. . . .

> The general tone of the team picked up immediately. It recovered its old-time solidarity, and once more the dogs leaped as one dog in the traces.

After time, however, the dogs tire from heavy loads. The dogs are sold to the Scotch half-breed who pushes the team harder than ever before. As leader, Buck is required to make sure that all dogs pull their weight.

> Buck did not like it, but he bore up well to the work, taking pride in it after the manner of Dave and Sol-leks, and seeing that his mates, whether they prided in it or not, did their fair share.

Throughout the toil of the trail, Buck maintains his pride, a sure sign of someone destined for greatness. The ability to keep his mental strength, even when his physical energy was sapped, is one thing that separates Buck from the other dogs. This fourth stage is symbolic of the human spirit, the intangible quality that allows the very few to achieve extremely high standards. It is this spirit that all humans possess, but only few can manifest its power. It is clear that Buck possessed this "human" spirit. In his battle with Spitz, a turning point in the novel, Buck uses more than just his physical attributes to defeat his rival:

Once Buck went over, and the whole circle of sixty dogs started up; but he recovered himself, almost in mid air, and the circle sank down again and waited.

But Buck possessed a quality that made for greatness— imagination. He fought by instinct, but he could fight by head as well.

In the first sentence, London illustrates Buck's fierce determination. Most other dogs would have simply accepted their fate, and impending death. However, Buck never gives up, and is able to right himself before any harm befalls him. In the second sentence we see another facet of his spirit, that of imagination. It is this quality, according to London, to which much of Buck's uniqueness is due. It is this quality which is the most human of any characteristic. Imagination is what sets humans apart from other animals, yet Buck is said to possess this characteristic. This is another example of London's human allegory, in which Buck is portrayed as being more than just an average dog. He is described as having that intangible which guides him through the fifth stage.

SYMBOLIC DEATH

In the fifth stage, Buck undergoes a period of symbolic death which he must overcome in order to proceed. This occurs during his relationship with Hal, Charles, and Mercedes, tenderfoots unaware of proper dog-sled procedure. Hal overloads the sled, pushes the dogs for too many miles, and doesn't ration their food. All of this adds up to worn, exhausted dogs on the verge of death. Although Buck is in supreme physical condition, he is also on the brink of death:

And through it all Buck staggered along at the head of the team as in a nightmare. He pulled when he could; when he could no longer pull, he fell down and remained down till blows from whip or club drive him to his feet again. All the stiffness and gloss had gone out of his beautiful furry coat. The hair hung down, limp and draggled, or matted with dried blood where Hal's club had bruised him. His muscles had wasted away to knotty strings, and the flesh pads had disappeared, so that each rib and every bone in his frame were outlined cleanly through the loose hide that was wrinkled in folds of emptiness. It was heart-breaking, only Buck's heart was unbreakable.

In this passage, we see a broken, weary Buck who hasn't the energy to even move. Once a powerful leader of a dog-sled team, he is now weak and fragile. This is the most vulnerable that we have seen Buck in the entire novel. He is as close to death, both literally and symbolically, as an animal can come. The only thing keeping him alive is his unbreakable heart. This indefatigable spirit is associated with humans, and provides another example of London's allegory. This symbolic death occurs in the lives of humans, during a crisis which marks the turning point in their lives. It is from this point where they begin to climb the mountain to self-fulfillment. It is from this critical event where they draw their inspiration. Buck's stout heart has enabled him to live through "death" and continue on to the sixth stage.

SYMBOLIC REBIRTH

The sixth stage encompasses Buck's rebirth and his journey towards apotheosis. It is during this stage that his relationship with John Thornton begins. It is John Thornton who pulls Buck from "death" by taking him from Hal, Mercedes, and Charles. However, while many other dogs died in the care of the tenderfoots, Buck's spirit enabled him to survive. As time progresses, Buck regains his strength and, with the help of Thornton's love, grows stronger and more powerful than he ever was. We begin to see that Buck is no longer just a dog; he performs feats unthinkable for his kind. In this scene, Buck pulls a sled weighing a thousand pounds for a distance of one hundred yards. Men bet thousands of dollars against Thornton, but Buck's spirit yet again triumphs:

> Buck threw himself forward, tightening the traces with a jarring lunge. His whole body was gathered compactly together in the tremendous effort, the muscles writhing and knotting like live things under the silky fur. His great chest was low to the ground, his head forward and down, while his feet were flying like mad, the claws scarring the hard-packed snow in parallel grooves. The sled swayed and trembled, half-started forward. One of his feet slipped, and one man groaned aloud. Then the sled lurched ahead in what appeared a succession of jerks, though it never really came to a dead stop again . . . half an inch . . . an inch . . . two inches. . . . The jerks perceptibly diminished; as the sled gained momentum, he caught them up, till it was moving steadily along.

In this scene, Buck performs an incomprehensible feat, one that goes beyond the imagination of its onlookers. "Men gasped and began to breathe again, unaware that for a moment they had ceased to breathe". It is in this scene that London confirms that Buck is more than a dog. He has not yet reached apotheosis, since he is still of flesh and blood, but he has proven that he is worthy of the seventh and final stage. Buck has symbolized the powerful human spirit throughout the novel, and continues to do so in this scene. Buck's will and determination, long recognized as human characteristics, are evident in this exciting scene. Buck has shown throughout the novel that he merits entry into the seventh stage.

DEIFICATION

Having paid his dues in life, Buck finally reaches apotheosis, and lives in the minds of all who knew him. Buck leaves the camp one day, only to [return to] find Thornton slain by a tribe of the Yeehat Indians. Buck exacts his revenge upon the Yeehats by killing their chief and several warriors. His rage clouds his thinking, and thus it is later that he contemplates his actions:

> At times, when he paused to contemplate the carcasses of the Yeehats, he forgot the pain of it; and at such times he was aware of a great pride in himself—a pride greater than any he had yet experienced. He had killed man, the noblest game of all, and he had killed in the face of the law of club and fang.

It is at this point that we realize that Buck has reached apotheosis. His link with the terrestrial world is thus broken, enabling him to enter into apotheosis. Not only has he mastered the society in which he lives, but he has conquered it. He has taken the rules and laws of his culture, and stood up to them, only to have them back down. It is at this point that he realizes that he has conquered society:

> They had died so easily. It was harder to kill a husky dog than them. They were no match at all, were it not for their arrows and spears and clubs. Thenceforward he would be unafraid of them except when they bore in their hands their arrows, spears, and clubs.

It is in this passage that Buck realizes that he has beaten society, and that he has become elevated above it. The allegory in this instance is a bit more subtle, in that humans aren't generally regarded as gods. However, the fact that Buck has overcome the obstacles of society and prospered is in itself a human allegory. Man attempts his best to make his mark in the world just as Buck did. The desire to be the very best is a human characteristic which Buck exemplifies, and the allegorical implications are clear.

Buck's apotheosis is complete when he is woven into the Indian folklore. After killing many warriors in a tribe of the

Yeehats, Buck is made into a superhuman character. "Then a panic seized the Yeehats, and they fled in terror to the woods, proclaiming as they fled the advent of the Evil Spirit". London further accentuates his point with his description of Buck as the Ghost Dog:

> And here may well end the story of Buck. The years were not many when the Yeehats noted a change in the breed of timber wolves; for some were seen with splashes of brown on head and muzzle, and with a rift of white centering down the chest. But more remarkable than this, the Yeehats tell of a Ghost Dog that runs at the head of the pack. They are afraid of this Ghost Dog, for it has cunning greater than they, stealing from their camps in fierce winters, robbing their traps, slaying their dogs, and defying their bravest hunters.

In this passage, Buck has made the step into the supernatural. He is no longer in the lives of the humans but in their imaginations. He has evolved into a figure of lore and memory and God-like attributes; he has truly undergone apotheosis. Similarly, the greatest humans of our times are immortalized in fashions such as this. Stories are told of their exploits, and the young are informed of their accomplishments. In this sense, the human allegory of *The Call of the Wild* holds true yet again.

In his *The Call of the Wild*, Jack London produced one of the greatest novels ever written. Besides his beautiful descriptions, and captivating plot, London wrote something that greatly appealed to the people of the world. He was able to capture the true spirit of man, and embody that spirit in his canine character of Buck. His reasons for this choice were clear: Using Buck, he could illustrate his point more easily and less awkwardly than if his character were human. London took us through his seven stages to apotheosis which applied both literally to Buck, and symbolically to humankind. By looking at the novel from this angle, we gain a better perspective on Buck, Jack London, and ourselves. It is the knowledge that we gain when reading *The Call of the Wild* that makes it such a classic. Critics are finally realizing what the people of the world have known for over eighty years; *The Call of the Wild* is an American and world classic.

WORKS CITED

Labor, Earle. *Jack London*. New York: Twayne, 1974.

Labor, Earle. "Jack London's Mondo Cane: The Call of the Wild and White Fang." *Jack London Newsletter 1* (1967): 2–13.

London, Jack. *The Call of the Wild.* Chicago: Nelson Hall, 1980.

"Naturalism." Holman, C. Hugh. *A Handbook to Literature,* Indianapolis: Bobbs-Merrill Fourth Edition, 1980.

Tavernier-Courbin, Jacqueline. *Critical Essays on Jack London.* Boston: G.K. Hall, 1983.

WORKS CONSULTED

Clayton, Lawrence. "The Ghost Dog: A Motif in *The Call of the Wild.*" *Jack London Newsletter 5* (1972): 158.

Hedrick, Joan D. *Solitary Comrade: Jack London and His Work.* Chapel Hill: The University of North Carolina Press, 1982.

London, Joan. *Jack London and His Times.* Seattle: University of Washington Press, 1968.

Lundquist, James. *Jack London: Adventures, Ideas, and Fiction.* New York: Ungar, 1987.

Watson, Charles N., Jr. *The Novels of Jack London.* Madison, Wisconsin: The University of Wisconsin Press, 1983.

Wilcox, Earl J. "Jack London's Naturalism: The Example of *The Call of the Wild.*" *Jack London Newsletter 2* (1969): 91–101.

The Wolf as a Symbol

Ann Upton

The image of the wolf, especially as found in London's books *The Call of the Wild* and *White Fang*, offers layer upon layer of meaning, observes essayist Ann Upton. London's identification with the animal—he even liked to be called "Wolf"—provides an illuminating look at the two sides of the author's nature.

If one were painting or sculpting Jack London as the old Greek gods were pictured with their animals, London's companion would, of course, be the wolf. He signed his letters "Wolf"; he called his never-occupied, great stone castle "Wolf House"; he once had a great, grey wolf as a pet; a wolf's head adorned his book marks; wolves frequently appear as characters in his novels and short stories and the word "wolf" itself often appears in the titles of many. How does one explain London's attraction to this animal? What was there in his own personality that responded instinctively to the wolf-image?

ARCHETYPAL IMAGES

There is, first, the archetypal image of the wolf as both preserver and destroyer, embodying the two conflicting wishes of mankind, the life wish and the death wish. In the story of creation according to Norse mythology, the sun and the moon are pursued by a pack of wolves which try to devour them and thus end everything. The wolf is also a creature of Odin, feasting on the slain and haunting the warrior paradise with one great, grey wolf watching the abode of the gods like Fate, knowing his time will come. Yet, as a creature dedicated to Odin, the giver of victory, the wolf is also a propitious sign. In Greek mythology, where everything was conceived in the likeness of man or beast, the wolf is the destructive principle; but by carrying away the old and unfit, he made way for new life and thus shared in the creative

Reprinted from Ann Upton, "The Wolf in London's Mirror," *Jack London Newsletter*, vol. 6, no. 3, September–December 1973.

function.[1] In Celtic myth, the wolf-dog (destroyer) is associated with the stag-god (preserver), and here the association is clearly that of life-and-death-upon-one-tether.[2] From our pastoral ancestors, we inherit the concept of the wolf as destroyer of the life-sustaining sheep. A "wolf in sheep's clothing" is also an image that dramatizes the difference between the appearance and the reality; it is a representation of the destroyer masked as the sustainer, and suggests the dual nature of all forces. Among the early agricultural tribes, according to Frazer in *The Golden Bough* (vol. 1, p. 270), the wolf was one of the embodiments of the corn-spirit which must be caught and killed in the last sheaf of corn so that the corn would come up next year. As the corn-spirit, the wolf was the sustainer of life so long as he was imprisoned in the corn; but escaped from control, he could be the destroyer by taking the spirit away from the corn and so preventing the food crop from growing the next year.

In the legend of Romulus and Remus, in the story of Mowgli in Rudyard Kipling's *Jungle Book*, and in some old Irish legends, the wolf becomes the preserver by suckling babies, imparting with the milk, perhaps, supernatural powers. Since London was never sure of the identity of his father, the adolescent fantasy of discovering one's "real" parents to be more admirable or desirable than the parents he lives with may have caused him to imagine them as animals and himself as a son of the wolf. In fact, in one of his first published stories, "Son of the Wolf," London has the Indians call all white men the sons of the wolf. The notion that a man can take on the form of a wolf has persisted from the time of older Roman writings (Petronius, in *The Satyricon*, relates one of the stories told at the banquet of Trimalchio of a man who turns into a wolf); through the loup-garou hysteria in sixteenth-century France when wolf-men, believed to have eaten children, were burned at the stake; to the *Dr. Jekyll and Mr. Hyde* of Robert Louis Stevenson. Whether London, familiar with these stories, selected the wolf image from them or whether he found the image in that collective unconscious psychologist Carl Jung claims we share is immaterial. It is his strong, consistent identification with the symbol that is intriguing.

1. H.R. Ellis Davidson, *Gods and Myths of Northern Europe* (Middlesex, England: Penguin Books, Ltd., 1964). 2. Anne Ross, *Pagan Celtic Britain* (London: Routledge and Kegan Paul, 1967), p. 341.

CONTEMPORARY INFLUENCES

Two contemporaneous influences that could have suggested the wolf image to London were the growing competitiveness of business and the gold rush in the Klondike. Idiomatic expressions using "wolf" fit in well with the competitive atmosphere of business in London's time. The "wolf at the door" and "to throw to the wolves" suggest that nineteenth century capitalism in its drive for profits was like a hungry wolf pack in search of food, a constant threat to the weak. A "lone wolf" carries the idea of independence, self-sufficiency— an idea in harmony with London's image of himself; but it also suggests a lack of social concern, a concept that London did not find so appealing and sought to remedy by his affiliation with the Socialist movement. "To wolf one's food" is to eat voraciously, to gobble up whatever in sight tempts one's appetite. In terms of the growing corporations, the application of the expression is clear; in terms of London personally, the expression had a sinister meaning which is discussed below.

As for the Klondike, that dream of wealth and adventure that drew so many men of London's age, one met there the wolf of myth and legend: the destroyer who was also cosmic energy, a heat force, the primal warmth amid all that desolate cold. Man could identify with this image and through the identification, renew his strength, courage, adaptability, *elan vital.*

Jack London, as a product of his time, could not have escaped the influence of these suggestions, nor the dichotomy of feeling generated by them. His innate perceptiveness, though, went farther, causing him to associate his own opposing sympathies with the two faces of the wolf. One London face—the adventurous, virile, combative, "natural" man face, typified by the blond, Anglo-Saxon Nietzschean superman—corresponded to the lone wolf, sufficient against the forces of nature in his universe, taking what he wanted, secure in his superiority. The other face—the friendship-seeking, justice-loving, intellectual product of education and civilization that sought expression in Socialism—was like the wolf when he ran in packs, answering the longing for brotherhood and mutual aid. In the wolf-symbol, then, were the two sides of London's nature united.

Through the use of this symbol, London was able to explore the depths of his own nature. A wild counterpart of the dog, the wolf has no structural differences from his domesticated brother. The only distinction between them is founded on their habits; wolves will even mate with larger domestic dogs. Thus it is easy for the wolf-dog to slip from civilization back to the primeval state as Buck does in *Call of the Wild*; or he may turn from the wild state to civilization as White Fang does [in *White Fang*]. Civilized man, even though he sees the primitive man in himself inadequately glossed over with civilization, can only play these interchangeable roles in dreams or fantasies. Yet by identifying with an animal which looks the same in both wild and domesticated states, he can vicariously journey from domestication into the primitive and back again. The journeys of London's two most famous dog-heroes are an attempt at vicarious atavism, and a mirror image of London's two faces.

Buck, in *Call of the Wild*, is the natural man, reverting to the primitive; the story concerns his experiences while learning to adapt to life's demands. The book ends when Buck is accepted into the wolf pack; he has successfully made the journey back to the roots of his nature. Buck's journey follows closely the journey of the hero as described by Joseph Campbell in *Hero with a Thousand Faces*. There is a call to adventure:

> Irresistible impulses seized [Buck] . . . He would be lying in camp, dozing lazily in the heat of day, when suddenly his head would lift and his ears cock up, intent and listening . . . seeking for the mysterious something that called—called waking or sleeping, at all times, for him to come.[3]

And the hero ventures forth from the common world into a region of supernatural wonder, the dark night of the soul, Dante's "dark wood":

> He sprang through the sleeping camp and in swift silence dashed through the woods. As he drew closer to the cry he went more slowly, with caution in every movement, till he came to an open place among the trees (*Call of the Wild*, p. 90).

Fabulous forces are there encountered and a decisive victory won:

> Looking out he saw, erect on haunches, with nose pointed to the sky, a long, lean timber wolf (*Call of the Wild*, p. 90).

There is, however, no victory in this encounter, for Buck does not go deep enough into the dark night or the dark forest:

3. Jack London, *The Call of the Wild and White Fang* (New Yolk: Bantam Pathfinder Editions, 1963), p. 89.

He knew he was at last answering the call, running by the side of his wood brother toward the place from where the call surely came . . . [but] Buck remembered John Thornton. He sat down . . . [then] turned about and started slowly on the back track (*Call of the Wild*, p. 91).

After Thornton's death, though, Buck answers the call again and this time he fights the whole wolf pack, winning the hero's decisive victory. Buck does not return as the hero should; he remains in the wild and we leave him running with the pack in the dark of the northern winter. If the light is consciousness, Buck is left in the depth of the unconscious. And here a strange parallel with London's life develops.

Jung has said that the archetype has a distinctly numinous character; it drives with remorseless logic to its goal and draws the subject under its spell.[4] The subject is at first unwilling, then no longer able to free himself. It is as though London drew from his unconscious the wolf-dog figure to answer by proxy his call to adventure, then the wolf-dog began to draw him. London said that, unlike his other writing which was laborious, *Call of the Wild* seemed to write itself, the story unfolding like an effortless slipping into unconsciousness. The experience should have brought a depth and fullness of meaning to both London and his archetypal hero, as Campbell says it brings to the hero who is enriched by his adventure and returns with power to bestow boons. But what happens to Buck? His adventure is aborted. London reaches the depths through his proxy, but he can't or won't find his way back, hence he cannot complete the second half of the hero's life, the assimilating of the unconscious potential gained in the symbolic journey. Buck stays in the younger world, reborn to primitive instincts, but dead to the conscious world.

WHITE FANG: THE COMPLETION OF THE HERO'S JOURNEY

London, like Buck, is a product of the South and civilization, and as he fights to survive, he learns as Buck does that when he sounds the "deeps of his nature . . . parts of his nature . . . [are] deeper than he, going back to the womb of Time" (*Call of the Wild*, p. 49). London, like Buck, leaves California and travels north to the Arctic Circle, finding successive depths of his nature as he travels north. Unlike Buck, however, he

---

4. Carl Jung, *The Basic Writings of C. G. Jung*, ed. Violet Staub de Laszle (New York: Modern Library, 1959), p. 75.

cannot stay in the wild. Jung says that "consciousness struggles in a regular panic against being swallowed up in the primitivity and unconsciousness of sheer instinctuality. . . . The closer one comes to the instinct world, the more violent is the urge to shy away from it. . . . Psychologically, however, the archetype as an image of instinct is a spiritual goal toward which the whole nature of man strives" (*Basic Writings*, p. 82). London, of course, had not yet read Jung (since *Call of the Wild* was published in 1903 and the first translations of Jung's writings appeared in the United States in 1916), but what he does with Buck and White Fang bears out the truth of Jung's observation. Wishing to leave a part of himself in the wild, or being urged by his nature both to stay and to go, London creates a surrogate to return to the conscious world—White Fang. White Fang makes his first voluntary move toward civilization when he goes back to Grey Beaver after spending a cold and lonely night at the deserted Indian campsite. He has sat in the center of the space Grey Beaver's tent has occupied, pointed his nose at the moon, and uttered his first long wolf-howl, a howl containing all "his apprehensions of sufferings and dangers to come."[5] With the coming of daylight, he decides to set out on "The Trail of the Gods." When he finally curls up by Grey Beaver's fire, and is fed, he is content, "secure in the knowledge that the morrow would find him, not wandering forlorn through bleak forest-stretches, but . . . with the gods to whom he had given himself" (*White Fang*, p. 194). Physical comforts, companionship, an object to worship—all have a part in his choosing civilization at this time.

Later, though, with Weedon Scott, White Fang's choice is tantamount to obligation, and seems to be more of a turning toward death than a return to consciousness. It is true that he travels to the south and warmth, but the old wild ecstasy is missing. In one of the early chapters of the book, killing the ptarmigan,

> [White Fang] was too busy and happy to know that he was happy. . . . He was thrilling and exulting. . . . The pitch to which he was aroused was tremendous. All the fighting blood of his breed was up in him and surging through him. This was living, though he did not know it (*White Fang*, p. 158).

And even when White Fang is being tormented by Beauty

5. *Call of the Wild and White Fang.* Hereafter references to either *Call of the Wild* or *White Fang* are to the edition cited in footnote three.

Smith, "The mere sight of Beauty Smith was sufficient to send him into transports of fury" (*White Fang*, p. 229). The word "transports" here suggests rapture—a pinnacle of living. It is reminiscent of the passage in [London's] *The Sea Wolf* when Humphrey Van Weyden wonders why Wolf Larsen does not kill the sailor, Leach, who hates him so. Larsen explains:

> It gives a thrill to life. . . . Why should I deny myself the joy of exciting Leach's soul to fever pitch? For that matter, I do him a kindness. . . . He is living more royally than any man for'ard . . . he is living deep and high. I doubt that he has ever lived so swiftly and keenly before, and I honestly envy him sometimes when I see him raging at the summit of passion and sensibility.[6]

It is hate that arouses this passion, but it is a life-passion.

Significantly, London titles the chapter in *White Fang*, in which comes the real turning point for White Fang, "The Clinging Death." The Clinging Death is a bull dog with whom White Fang fights. The dog does not fight like any animal White Fang has ever known. He waddles in good naturedly, never seems to become aroused, gets a grip on White Fang's throat and holds on, slowly squeezing the life out of him. The bull dog, as impersonal as a force of nature, motivated neither by the thrill of battle nor the desire for life, subdues White Fang. After this, White Fang's hold on life seems loosened, for Weedon Scott rescues him, becomes his new god and demands of him, through love, the final obligation of any god—death. White Fang follows Weedon Scott south and the reader leaves White Fang lying "with half-shut, patient eyes, drowsing in the sun."

Compare that with the last glimpse of Buck:

> When the long winter nights come on and the wolves follow their meat into the lower valleys, he may be seen running at the head of the pack through the pale moonlight or glimmering borealis, leaping gigantic above his fellows, his great throat a-bellow as he sings a song of the younger world, which is the song of the pack.

There is poetry and vigor in the expression of the earlier book, while by the end of *White Fang*, even the style seems to drowse. Clearly, White Fang's journey is toward a more subdued life (if not death) while Buck's is toward a more in-

6. Jack London, *The Sea Wolf and Selected Stories* (New York: The New American Library, Inc.. 1964), p. 121.

tense one. Yet London himself thought *White Fang* the better book. It may be that he was trying to prove something to himself, or to justify his own return.

EERIE PROPHECY

Then does London's return from the Klondike follow the pattern of White Fang's journey? London comes out sick, needing in order to sustain life, the fresh foods of the South and civilization. He . . . may only have been completing the journey of the hero. His return, however, is not the triumphant hero's return: he fails to bring back the boon he sought—the elixir that restores the world. For London, the "stinging things of the spirit" are gone. When he tries to recapture them in Socialism, in women, in fame or security, he fails; only in his stories of the far North does he approach the early ecstasy of life. Later, in the autobiographical *Martin Eden*, London makes his dark journey of withdrawal from the external to the internal world; when he retreats to the peace within, he regresses to what Jung calls the infantile unconscious. And to make the analogy even stronger, Martin Eden (London's surrogate), apathetic, finding life an intolerable burden, slips into the sea and drowns himself. In Jungian symbolism the sea stands for the womb, so that in effect Jack London, through his character Martin Eden, finishes his hero's quest by deciding life is not worth living and returning to the womb. In terms of London's own life it is eerily prophetic.

Prophetic also is the emphasis in *White Fang* on the law of survival: "Eat or be eaten." As Maxwell Geismar in *Rebels and Ancestors* says of *White Fang*: "All love, affection, sense of trust [is reduced] to an oral context, stronger, more continuous and basic than the sexual drive itself. The law of life became only and purely the law of meat." When White Fang's father, old One Eye, is stalking the lynx, he watches as the lynx lies crouched, waiting for a porcupine to open himself up. Wolf, lynx, and porcupine are all "intent on life; and such was the curiousness of the game, the way of life for one lay in eating the other and the way of life for the other lay in not being eaten" (*White Fang*, p. 145). In fact, London repeats the law "eat or be eaten" so often that he apparently convinces himself; for when he is 40, overweight, and sick with uremia, he continues to eat two raw ducks a day. It is reminiscent of the man in London's story "Love of Life" who stuffs his mattress with food because he has once been so hungry. But it is also a way of using the wolf's voracious appetite to eat oneself to death.

London certainly felt a deep instinctual identification with the wolf-dog figures in *Call of the Wild* and *White Fang*. Van Wyck Brooks called it London's "literary lycanthropy." Sidney Alexander[7] claims Jack London wasn't sure whether he was a man or a wolf. Although this assertion does seem a trifle exaggerated, it does indicate how deeply every London reader feels this identification and how remarkable was London's insight into his own character to choose and develop this image.

7. Sidney Alexander, "Jack London's Literary Lycanthropy," *Reporter*, 16 (1957), 46–48.

CHAPTER 3

Autobiographical Roots in *The Call of the Wild*

READINGS ON
THE CALL OF THE WILD

Buck and His Creator Were Both Unfairly Jailed

Andrew Flink

When young Jack London was illegally arrested for vagrancy and sentenced to thirty days in jail without even being allowed to enter a plea, he became violently angry. But, as he reported in the "Pinched" and "The Pen" sections of his book *The Road*, that month in the penitentiary taught him survival skills in a brutish world, forcing him to hide his anger and adapt to an inhuman society. According to Andrew Flink, author of the following viewpoint, London drew deeply on those experiences in writing *The Call of the Wild*. Flink compares the experiences of real-life young man and fictional dog to find the sources for London's powerful descriptions of Buck's saga.

> I plead guilty, but I was unconscious of it at the time. I did not mean to do it.[1]

So spoke Jack London about his most enduring novel, *Call of the Wild*. He was, of course, referring to the underlying story-behind-the-story that some saw as human allegory. Along these lines, James Glennon Cooper made the observation that

> London put many things into his stories he did not mean to include. Conscious intention and unconscious accomplishment were often far apart . . .[2]

and

> The breaching of the barrier between the consciousness and the unconscious once accomplished, allows more and more images to emerge from the depths of the unconscious.[3]

---

1. Joan London, *Jack London and His Times: An Unconventional Biography* (Seattle, University of Washington Press, 1968), p. 252. 2. James Glennon Cooper, "The Womb of Time: Archetypal Patterns in the Novels of Jack London," *Jack London Newsletter*, 8:2 (1975). 3. Ibid.

Reprinted from Andrew Flink, "*Call of the Wild*—Jack London's Catharsis," *Jack London Newsletter*, vol. 11, no. 1, January–April 1978. Reprinted by permission of the author.

In Jack London's life his sensitivity was assailed by two major events, the rejection of fatherhood by Chaney, a subject I touched on in *"Call of the Wild*—Parental Metaphor," *Jack London Newsletter* 7:57 (1974), and the experience of the Erie County Penitentiary both of which seemed to be highly traumatic for him. The Erie County experience, shock that it was, became the turning point of his life, steering him to education and ultimately to writing.

It's interesting to note, however, that while John Thornton seemed to be a parental metaphor, the story of Buck, before meeting John Thornton, might well be considered a "writing out" of the Erie County experience. With this in mind I'd like to take you on an excursion that might prove interesting by pointing up some parallels that exist between London's experiences in Erie County and Buck's experiences after being taken from the ranch in Santa Clara. In view of London's statement that he was "unaware of what he'd done" and in keeping with James Glennon Cooper's viewpoint about the unconscious, I'm going to proceed on the idea that London wasn't aware, cite some examples of why I think so and let you decide.

PHYSICAL SIMILARITIES

First, London's description of Buck is very much a description of London himself. From *War of the Classes* we read London's own words: "I was healthy and strong, bothered with neither aches or weaknesses,"[4] and [had] "a stomach that could digest scrap iron and a body which flourished on hardships."[5]

He describes Buck: "His muscles became hard as iron and he grew callous to all ordinary pain," or "He could eat anything, no matter how loathsome or indigestible."[6]

London's description of Buck coincides clearly with what he'd written of himself.

Add to this the following reference to Buck's age on page 18 of *Call of the Wild*: "During the four years since his puppyhood . . ."

One year in the life of a human is seven for a dog. This would make Buck twenty-eight human years old, London was twenty-seven when he finished Buck's story.

---

4. Jack London, *War of the Classes* (N.Y., Macmillan, 1905), p. 268. 5. Ibid., p. 270. 6. Jack London, *Call of the Wild* (N.Y., Macmillan, 1903), p. 61. All other references to this novel will immediately follow the quotation.

SIMILAR EXPERIENCES

From the beginning of *Call of the Wild*, London touched on a common denominator between his brilliant novel and the Erie County experience. Manuel's treachery was the turning point in Buck's easygoing life of a ranch dog. Taken from the ranch, he's suddenly thrown into a situation completely foreign and strange to him. His freedom is curtailed, and he's exposed to cruelty and barbaric treatment. In "Pinched," London finds himself in much the same situation, freedom suddenly curtailed leading to the inhumanity he witnessed as a convict.

Buck was sold to pay a gambling debt with which he had no connection. London was arrested to pay a debt he felt he never incurred. Both were victims of money, Buck sold to pay a gambling debt, London "was nabbed by a fee hunting constable."[7]

"Buck accepted the rope [placed around his neck by Manuel] with quiet dignity" (p. 20) and with faith in the way of things to go fair and just. London, by the same token, allowed himself to be taken to jail with the idea in mind that he could present his case and justice would prevail. In *The Road* London states:

> He'd have never run after me, [the arresting officer] for two hoboes in the hand are worth more than one on the getaway. But like a dummy I stood still when he halted me.[8]

Later, London's eyes were opened wider by the facts. He was sentenced to thirty days by a biased and unfeeling court—only thirty days, but a month that would force a decision out of him that was to affect the rest of his life.

In "Pinched" London faces the reality of jail—he was behind bars! He describes the holding cell.

> "The hobo" is that part of a prison where the minor offenders were confined [together] in a large iron cage.[9]

Buck, after leaving Manuel, is placed in a crate and there he stayed until the dog taming sequence by the man in the red sweater. The visions of bars were common between the two situations. London states it as: "[Buck] raged at them through the bars" (p. 24).

While in the "hobo" London said that "here we met several hoboes who had already been pinched this morning, and every little while the door was unlocked and two more were thrust in on us."[10]

---

7. *War of the Classes*, op. cit., p. 276. 8. Jack London, *The Road* (N.Y., Macmillan, 1907), p. 76. 9. Ibid., p. 77. 10. *The Road*, op. cit., p. 77.

Buck witnessed a situation that was similar: "As the days went by, other dogs came, in crates and at the ends of ropes, some docilely, and some raging and roaring as he [Buck] had come" (p. 33).

To this point there would seem to be a close parallel between the experiences suffered by Buck and by London. The visions of bars in the crate where Buck was imprisoned and the implication of bars described by London in "Pinched" as "a large iron cage" follow closely with each other. A relationship would certainly seem to exist. Here are some more examples:

London was transferred with other convicts to Buffalo by train from Niagara Falls. Buck also was transferred among other ways, by train.

States London: "Down the streets of Niagara Falls we were marched to the railroad station, stared at by curious passers-by." [11]

London and the others were, like Buck, placed on the train. London writes that "[Buck] was trucked off the steamer into a great railway depot, and finally he was deposited in an express car" (p. 25).

Like London, who was subjected to shame by the people of Niagara Falls and who felt "afire with indignation . . . at the outrage," [12] Buck also felt "the more outrage to his dignity and his anger waxed and waxed" (p. 24).

Later, when his indignation cooled, London began to settle down to the task of survival in Erie County; Buck likewise had the same change of heart. London says: "My indignation ebbed away and into my being rushed the tides of fear. I saw at last clear-eyed, what I was up against." [13]

SETTLING DOWN TO SURVIVAL

Buck echoes: "He was beaten (he knew that); but he was not broken. He saw, once for all, that he stood no chance against a man with a club. He had learned the lesson, and in all his after life he never forgot it" (p. 32).

Could this last sentence be the key to this entire idea? London left Erie County with the avowed intention of getting an education, to "open the books," and later to become a writer. He never forgot the Erie County experience, speaking of it later in years as "unprintable and unthinkable," describing it

11. Ibid., p. 82. 12. Ibid., p. 83. 13. Ibid., p. 97.

in "Pinched" as "unbelievable and monstrous"[14] and writing it years later into *Call of the Wild* with the following: "The facts of life took on a fiercer aspect; and while he faced that aspect uncowed, he faced it with all the latent cunning of his nature aroused" (pp. 32–33).

While in Erie County London certainly did face it with "all the latent cunning of his nature aroused." He became a trustee and gained some degree of autonomy, however small. But the gnawing spectre of hunger seemed to be a major problem and food was hard to come by.

> We were a hungry lot in the Erie County Pen. . . .
>
> I used to steal their grub while serving them. Man cannot live on bread alone and not enough of it.[15]

Buck's problem was similar: "So greatly did hunger compel him, he was not above taking what did not belong to him" (p. 59).

From London's assessment that what he encountered was "unprintable and unthinkable" and that he, according to Charmian, had understated the case in what she refers to as "a hint of what he calls the 'unprintable' details"[16] either consciously or unconsciously, London must have been reliving the Erie County experience as he wrote *Call of the Wild*. What he experienced must have been a great shock. Imagine the effect of the kind of brutality described in "Pinched" and "The Pen" on someone as sensitive as London and who had the compassion for people that he had—one can only imagine what horrors he saw that he didn't write about. This along with the fact that he was only eighteen when he lived this experience—it must have made an indelibly deep impression and, like Buck, "in all his after life he never forgot it" (p. 32).

The depth of the impression might be measured with the following from "The Pen":

> There was a young Dutch boy, about eighteen years of age, who had fits most frequently. . . .
>
> He prefaced his fits with howling. He howled like a wolf.[17]

Compare that with what Buck witnessed: "Dolly, who had never been conspicuous for anything, went suddenly mad. She announced her condition by a long, heart-breaking wolf howl that sent every dog bristling with fear" (p. 78).

Immediately after being taken into custody, London's

---

14. Ibid. 15. Ibid., p. 99. 16. Charmian London, *Book of Jack London* (N.Y., Century Co., 1921), I:185. 17. *The Road*, op. cit., p. 115.

confusion as to why he was there became very evident as seen from this example from *The Road*:

> I was forced to toil hard on a diet of bread and water and to march the shameful lock-step with armed guards over me—and all for what? What had I done? What crime had I committed against the good citizens of Niagara Falls that all this vengeance should be wreaked upon me? I had not even violated their "sleeping-out" ordinance. I had slept outside their jurisdiction in the county that night, I had not even begged for a meal, or bartered for a "light piece" on their streets. All I had done was to walk along their sidewalk and gaze at their picayune waterfall and what crime was there in that?
>
> . . . I wanted to send for a lawyer. The guard laughed at me. So did the other guards. I really was incommunicado.[18]

Buck was equally confused:

> There he lay for the remainder of the weary night, nursing his wrath and wounded pride. He could not understand what it all meant. What did they want with him, these strange men? Why were they keeping him pent up in this narrow crate? He did not know why, but he felt oppressed by a vague sense of impending calamity. Several times during the night he sprang to his feet when the shed door rattled open expecting to see the Judge, or the boys at least. But each time it was the bulging face of the saloonkeeper that peered in at him by the sickly light of a tallow candle (pp. 23–24).

London's statement about being incommunicado would seem to match up with the implied incommunicado state experienced by Buck.

SYMBOLIC BIRTH

Buck's overwater voyage from Seattle to Dyea reads like a symbolic birth from London's tramp existence and its restless uncertainty of what his future held, to a definite plan with accompanying goals.

> When the heroes of *Call of the Wild*, *Nostromo*, and *Moby-Dick* must each cross a body of water in a small conveyance, the event represents a common "unconscious core" in the minds of the authors. The body of water reflected from this core represents the point of separation between life and death, but the cask and water of the exposure myth become the womb and the amniotic fluid in which the fetus grows to birth.[19]

The release from Erie County brought a new awareness to Jack London. It not only gave him a clearer picture of the brutalities of life, but it also made him want to do something about it. The difficulties ahead (to become a writer) were formidable. In [the *Call of the Wild* chapter] "Dominant Primordial Beast," London wrote a paragraph that almost seems to be the essence of London himself at the point in time when he wrote *Call of the Wild*. He'd found his niche, he was moderately successful and maybe even elated:

> There is an ecstasy that marks the summit of life, and beyond which life cannot rise. And such is the paradox of living, this ecstasy comes when one is most alive, and it comes as a complete forgetfulness that one is alive. This ecstasy, this forgetfulness of living, comes to the artist, caught up and out of himself in a sheet of flame (p. 91).

To say in one of the strongest passages of the story that "the artist is caught up and out of himself" might well be leading into the very heart of the *Call of the Wild*, in which London "wrote out" his feelings about himself. This occurs early in the novel when Buck is learning to survive after the experience of the sellout by Manuel and the subsequent events. To this point London's psyche had been something very elusive to him and he said of himself: "I had been reborn but not renamed and I was running around to find out what manner of thing I was."[20]

Buck's case was worded differently but the content is the same: "He was sounding the depths of his nature, and of the parts of his nature that were deeper than he, going back into the Womb of Time" (p. 91).

It seems that each one, Buck and London, was searching for his own personal identification—London's search began upon his release from Erie County and culminating in his goal as a writer.[21] Buck's rebirth began in the north and with the struggle to survive eventually becoming [as he is described in the book's second-to-last paragraph] a "great, gloriously coated wolf, like, and yet unlike, all other wolves." London's struggle to become a writer must certainly have included self-evaluation as one means to an end. Again we have a significant phrase: "He was sounding the depths of his nature."

The significance for both Buck and London is carried farther and the idea reappears as the chapter titled "The Sounding of the Call." A repeated use of "sounding" and "depths" brings to mind not audible sound but rather sound

20. *War of the Classes*, op. cit., pp. 277–278. 21. Charmian London, op. cit., I:186.

as a means of measuring depth, in the same manner as river pilots used soundings as navigational aids.

Buck pursued

> the call . . . sounding in the depths of the forest. It filled him with a great unrest and strange desires. It caused him to feel a vague, sweet gladness, and he was aware of wild yearnings and stirrings for he knew not what. Sometimes he pursued the call into the forest, looking for it as though it were a tangible thing (p. 199).

There's an interesting phrase, pursuing the call as though it were tangible. Relate this phrase to one I mentioned earlier written by and about London from *War of the Classes*: "I was running around trying to find out what manner of thing I was." [22]

Buck followed the call into the forest in an attempt to take a "sounding of the call" in order to learn "what manner of thing I [London] was . . ."

What does all this mean? Maybe nothing! Then again it might mean that the *Call of the Wild* became the success it did because of the factors of: first, the trauma of Erie County, the nebulous parentage, and the fact that *Call of the Wild* was an autobiographical purging of the two strongest elements of his life up to the point of writing this haunting story, London's catharsis, as it were. This too could be one reason why the story just about wrote itself.

> It [*Call of the Wild*] got away from me, and instead of 4000 words it ran 32000 before I could call a halt. [23]

This might imply a kind of compulsion or a "pursuit of the call into the forest, looking for it as though it were a tangible thing," London's "conscious intention and unconscious accomplishment." [24]

What can we conclude from all this? Maybe these examples I've outlined might serve to pick out some pattern regarding London's creative powers. It would certainly tend to point up his sensitivity to his life's experiences and how they influenced his writing, either consciously or unconsciously. London's sensitivity was acute, his total recall a thing of wonder and the Erie County experience along with his parental problem became something for him to acknowledge and cope with—perhaps *Call of the Wild* is how he did it. His writings are laced with a restlessness and maybe this

22. *War of the Classes*, op. cit., pp. 277–278. 23. Charmian London, op. cit., I:388. 24. James Glennon Cooper, op. cit., *JLN*, 8:2 (1975).

too is significant in some way, as though he never felt secure in spite of his successes and the following his name attracted (and still attracts). I feel that London was "sounding the deeps of his nature" all through his life but especially during his life as a writer. Maybe there's some personal significance for him in this respect when he has Buck return to the site of John Thornton's death where "he muses for a time, howling once, long and mournfully, ere he departs" (p. 228).

Or that London felt the "sheer surging of life" (p. 91) by putting Buck's story on paper.

Jack London's "superb meteor, every atom in magnificent glow" was formed from the Erie County experience to the completion of *Call of the Wild*, the completion of which found him

> leaping gigantic above his [London's] fellows [a leading writer among writers], his great throat a-bellow [expressing himself as a writer in a strong voice and being heard] as he sings a song of the younger world, which is the song of the pack (p. 231).

The Call of the Wild Is an Attempted Escape from the Evils of Capitalism

Joan London

Jack London's daughter Joan writes that her father's Klondike adventures shook up his political beliefs. Like many people at the time, London embraced the ideals of socialism as the cure for the evils of capitalism. But the rigors of life in the Klondike offered a third possibility: an escape from capitalism through a return to nature. Between his return from the Klondike and his writing *The Call of the Wild* four years later, London visited the worst slums of London, England, and was appalled by the conditions in that city's East End, an experience that deepened his antipathy toward capitalism. *The Call of the Wild*, writes his daughter, represents his attempt to flee from the struggle for existence in a capitalist society while it paradoxically brought him capital success as a popular and (for future books) well-paid author.

The first half of 1897 seemed very placid. Few noticed either the gradual easing of the long depression or the war clouds that were beginning to form. But in the middle of the summer news of an event that had occurred nearly a year before threw the country into a fever of excitement which was to last, despite the Spanish-American War, for more than two years. Before the first of August the rush to the Klondike was on.

Reports of the gold strike found Jack at the end of his resources and wearily searching for another job with which to buy a few more months of leisure in which to write later in the fall. With every repetition of how a few Alaskan prospectors had walked off the SS *Portland* with three quarters of a million dollars in gold dust, his conviction grew that he, too, could make a fortune in the Klondike. Unfortunately, however, a decision to join the rush could not be carried out simply. . . . He would need an outfit and money.

Jack's frantic efforts to be grubstaked were like those of thousands of other impecunious young men throughout the nation. But the unprecedented madness which gripped young as well as older Americans at this time cannot be entirely explained by their lust for gold. Unexpectedly a new frontier had appeared. "There being no new oceans to explore," writes a poet, "the cry 'Bonanza!' roused the world-old zest!" Jack listened ardently. For two years and a half he had stayed at home, his wanderlust submerged in the grueling struggle to obtain an education and learn how to write. Now as he listened to tales of hardship and danger he saw the adventure path before him once more and knew that he must go. . . .

Help came from an unexpected quarter. Captain Shepard, his sister Eliza's elderly husband, caught the fever and gladly grubstaked him in exchange for his company on the trip. When the SS *Umatilla*, laden with gold seekers, left San Francisco on July twenty-fifth, they were aboard. . . .

FEW FOUND FORTUNE

Word of the strike [had] spread quickly down the Yukon to Forty-Mile and Circle City, and in a short time the old-timers had staked the Bonanza and adjacent creeks. . . . Before snow fell the new town of Dawson had come into existence on the wide, spruce-covered flat at the junction of the Klondike and the Yukon rivers. During the following spring and summer the remainder of the new El Dorado was quietly prospected and located by small efficient stampedes. When the first "chekakos" arrived the sourdoughs had the situation well in hand, and most of the newcomers were destined to get little besides the trip for their hardships, suffering and money.

In later years Jack London often quoted the old miner's adage that "two dollars go into the ground for each dollar that comes out," and observed that the Klondike was no exception. The approximate quarter of a million gold hunters who started for the North during the two big years of the rush spent in the aggregate a staggering sum for transportation, equipment and supplies. The rigors of the trip from salt water over the passes to the Yukon discouraged many. A scant fifty thousand reached the interior. An infinitesimal percentage of these brought back fortunes of varying sizes; among the less than one seventh who actually found any gold at all, a few broke even.

Jack found no gold in the Klondike. Winter closed in before he scarcely prospected at all. He performed no feats and had no adventures, save that of managing to get in before the freeze-up, for it came early that year and many were stranded en route. But from the time he landed on the beach at Dyea until he floated, scurvy ridden, down the Yukon on his way home the following spring, he was amassing a store of impressions of things heard and seen, which were to yield him a fortune during the succeeding years.

THE TRIP TO THE YUKON

The saga of Jack London's trip over the Chilkoot to the Yukon in the fall of '97 is the saga of the thousands who came then and later on the same errand. The steamers dumped their passengers and freight at low tide on a long sand spit opposite the Indian village of Dyea, and departed as quickly as possible. Long before all the boxes and bundles could be separated by their owners and lugged ashore through the shallow water the tide rose. Thousands of helpless argonauts and tons of baggage cluttered the beach. Behind them reared the snowy Coast Range Mountains which must be crossed, and immediately, if they hoped to reach Dawson that year. The small number of Indians and horses that were available could pack but a fraction of the stuff. They went to the highest bidder, and for the average man the price was soon out of sight. Many gave up without even trying, sold their equipment and took the next steamer home. Others started out manfully only to turn back, defeated.

While still aboard ship Jack and Captain Shepard had formed a partnership with three others. In the midst of the confusion they brought their outfit safely ashore, pitched camp and laid plans for the next move. Of the two passes, White and Chilkoot, the latter was the more difficult but appreciably shorter. Their choice was quickly made: they would start up Chilkoot in the morning. At this point Captain Shepard remembered that discretion was the better part of valor, and after listening to vivid descriptions of the difficult journey ahead, decided, much to Jack's relief, to return.

The trail led across several snowy plateaus, which grew rapidly steeper until inexperienced men, laden with packs, scrambled upon hands and knees to the foot of the pass. Many maintained that the Chilkoot was in no sense of the word a pass but a mountain itself. Those who ascended its precipitous thousand feet in two hours made excellent time. At one point the Indians had cut a thousand steps in the ice, but otherwise there was no path. From the top it was possible to coast down a short distance, then a new type of trail began which "Scotty" Allan, famous Alaskan dog driver, described as "a series of flats, mountains, hills, water, mud, quagmires and bogs from one end to the other."

Jack toiled zestfully with the rest. Daily he increased his load and knew pride when he could pack as well as the Indians. Even then, perhaps, he was beginning to be conscious of a personal ideal which later, after exposure to Nietzsche, would dominate much of his work. He visioned a certain type of white man who could equal the physical prowess of the finest specimens of primitive man, and outdo them, as well as his less favored white brothers, in intellectual power and achievement. As the years passed this became an obsession. Failing to realize it in himself, he began to weave his wish into his stories, where accomplishment was easy and sure.

On the Klondike trail in '97, however, he succeeded. In record time the four men reached Lake Linderman, the smallest of five glacial lakes which they would follow to the Lewes River and thence via the Pelly to the Yukon. Trees were felled at Linderman, cut into boards at the single small sawmill, and a boat was quickly constructed.

Jack had never been part of a struggle against such tremendous odds. The swift, sure approach of winter was daily more evident. The bitter winds against which they fought their way across the long lakes could not prevent ice from forming in sheltered pools, and no one could predict when the freeze-up would occur. They wasted no time in weighing their chances. Hour by hour they pushed forward, overcoming each obstacle as they came to it. Jack's skill in handling a small boat stood them in good stead, for the sail they rigged up, despite the weather, saved them many hours of rowing.

Linderman, Bennet, Tagish and Marsh—four of the lakes and their connecting passages were behind them when they

entered Fifty Mile River which at two points narrowed pre-
cipitately into the dreaded Box Canyon and White Horse
Rapids. Because portage would consume valuable time, Jack
ran the boat through both of them, avoiding disaster in the
whirlpool of the first and shooting down the foaming, wave-
like crest of the second. They knew that now they were past
the worst dangers, but at Lake Lebarge they encountered a
storm which forced them back for three days in succession.
On the fourth they made it, fighting across inch by inch and
watching the lake freeze behind them.

Dawson had been their destination, but when they
reached the Yukon word of a recent strike at the mouth of
the Stewart River, seventy miles short of Dawson, determined a change of plans. On October ninth, two and a half
months after they left San Francisco, they made camp on
Upper Island, between the Stewart and Henderson Creek.
And there, in one of several cabins which had been abandoned by Bering Sea fur traders, Jack's active participation
in the gold rush came to an end. . . .

THE WRITER'S TREASURE IS NOT GOLD

In later years Jack was fond of saying, "It was in the
Klondike that I found myself. There nobody talks. Everybody
thinks. You get your perspective. I got mine." The Klondike
gave much to Jack London, but it was the speech and not the
silence of his companions that enriched that gift. Night after
night during the long winter months of enforced idleness
men gathered together in the small warm cabins and talked.
And Jack listened.

At the time he did not know that what he was hearing,
combined with what he saw with his own eyes during visits
to Dawson and in camp on Upper Island, was story material.
Only toward the end of his stay did it occur to him that he
might be able to sell a few articles to the travel and outdoor
magazines. He listened and egged on the old-timers to further yarns because he was as interested in the new land as
any of the great audience at home. And while he satisfied his
curiosity the characters, scenes and incidents of scores of
short stories and several novels were being stored away.

Two months in Dawson during the early winter netted
him much. The raw frontier town appeared often in his later
books. And out of Dawson came Buck, the hero of the first
and greatest of his dog stories. He was fascinated by the

color and bombast of the mining town, so like those that had flourished in his own state nearly half a century before, but it was during the months in camp that he came to know the old Alaska of the sourdoughs and the Indians.

It was midwinter when he returned to Upper Island. On the shortest day of the year there were two hours of sunlight. Intense cold and what he was to call the "white silence" hemmed in the small group of men who awaited the coming of spring so that they might determine the worth of the claims they had staked near by. The camp was a cross section of the new life that was pulsing through Alaska. Many were newcomers, some from farm and city in the States, others chronic wanderers who had been in the South Seas the year before and might turn up on the docks of Liverpool the next. There were several who did not speak of their past and none asked them, but most were eager to swap experiences in the nightly gatherings.

Louis Savard's cabin, the largest and most comfortable on the island, was the favorite meeting place. Louis' French-Canadian accent so delighted Jack that he drew him into conversation at every opportunity. That accent runs musically through many of his stories and Louis himself appears, while Nig, his sled dog who so cleverly evaded hard work, became one of Buck's teammates in *The Call of the Wild*. . . .

He listened avidly to the adventures of men in their quest for gold, but whether on trail or in camp, it was the land itself that most deeply impressed him—and man's not always successful struggle to exist in it. Here the ancient battle for survival was expressed in its simplest terms. Hushed primeval forests and snowy wastelands, the austere blaze of the aurora borealis, the vast impersonal force of a land inimical to life—these dominate his first stories, and through them move those who had learned to survive in the pitiless environment, the Indians and the old-timers. Were it not for this awareness of man's ceaseless struggle against overwhelming odds, these would have been merely mediocre tales in which one-dimensional figures performed somewhat incredibly against a painted backdrop.

THE PROBLEM WITH CIVILIZATION IS CAPITALISM

The gold rush of which he was a part did not interest him, then. It was motivated by, and was bringing with it, much that he most despised in civilization. Eagerly he questioned the old-timers, and slowly the picture of Alaska in the days of the trail breakers grew in his mind. The early prospectors did not know that they were breaking trail. They had come, as they had often come before to far places, in response to the rumor of gold. Its promise, ever renewed, had held them fast through years of toil and suffering. Inured to hardship, else they would not have stayed, they had adapted themselves to the country, to its climate and its people. . . .

Nature alone was the enemy, indifferent to their strivings and dealing death impartially to all who relaxed their vigilance. And Jack, listening, saw the quiet years come and go; saw the toil-hardened miners and thrilled to the tale of their unsung deeds. . . .

He did not consciously deplore the coming of the new, but his admiration for the outmoded old was tinged with regret that such fine things should pass. Sick of civilization as he had found it, life in the brief years before [gold was discovered in the Klondike] seemed Arcadian. Then, courage, strength and intelligence, not a bank balance, had determined the status of men. Weakness, cowardice and greed, protected and perpetuated by wealth in civilization, were swiftly eliminated by nature, Indian tribal law and simple frontier justice. As he recalled life in the States his conviction grew that in the wilds men bulked larger as men than when penned in cities, were freer, nobler, more admirable.

And yet, although it flowered in cities, he knew that civilization was inherently good, not bad. Through it man had escaped his long thralldom to precisely what he was witnessing in Alaska, the endless, full-time struggle against nature just to keep alive. It was bad now because of capitalism. Once the producing class rose in its might, destroyed its masters and won to socialism, life would be fair beyond dreams. But now? And in the meantime? He drew back, shuddering, from the trap whose teeth he had seen and felt.

PAINFUL INDECISION

Thus, imperceptibly at first, the problem he was never to solve for himself took form during the winter on Upper Island. If he had come to Alaska before he had "opened the books" at all, or if, instead of too much Rousseau and too little Marx and large hunks of undigested Darwin, he had been well grounded in both science and socialism, the impact of the frontier would not have thrown him off balance. As it was, the widening of his horizon brought confusion rather than greater clarity.

He was a simple, direct man, and his need for simplicity was urgent. Things were good or bad, black or white, and thus he chose. But when he was confronted with a third choice his indecision was painful. He had aligned himself on the side of socialism rather than accept capitalism, and had been content. Now in the Klondike he found a third possibility which seemed to offer an escape from the evils of civilization by a return to nature.

What he feared and hated under capitalism did not obtain on the frontier. Its simplicity attracted him enormously. Furthermore, it already existed, was tangible, did not have to be attained by bloody struggle through many years. It had its drawbacks, but could they not be remedied by judicious borrowing of efficiency and comforts from civilization? And could not one fight for socialism even more effectively when his strength was not dissipated by close contact with capitalism's festering cities? Certainly, he would rationalize enthusiastically, the virtues of the frontier, doomed to perish under capitalism, should be preserved, and how better to accomplish this than by celebrating them out of one's own intimate knowledge?

He was never to frame these questions nor openly make the decision they posed, but from the time he returned from Alaska until the end of his life, he sought with growing desperation to reconcile his revolutionary principles and belief in the class struggle with his personal desires and preferences. The actual conflict was bitter and brief. In less than a decade the fatal combination of his spectacular rise to fame and affluence, his incomplete knowledge of Marxism, and the backwardness of the American socialist movement spelled defeat for his principles. Thereafter preference ruled, brilliantly rationalized, but transparent finally even to himself.

But as he emerged from the Klondike in the spring of '98, ill, penniless, and facing new responsibilities at home, no foreshadowing of future glory or ultimate disillusionment marked his bleak horizon. He had intended to remain in the North at least through the summer. If his Henderson Creek claim failed to pan out he would seek elsewhere. But long before spring released the land for prospecting he had been gripped by scurvy, which grew steadily worse until a return to fresh vegetables became imperative. Furthermore, the first mail in the spring had brought him news of [his stepfather] John London's death the preceding October, and he knew that Flora [his mother] would need him. Early in June he left Dawson with two companions, and in a rowboat floated fifteen hundred miles down the Yukon to salt water, and thence by steamer, stoking, to Seattle. On the last leg of the journey he returned to the road, beating his way, sharply aware of the absence of the exhilaration that had always accompanied similar feats in the past, on fast passenger trains to Oakland.

He was in no cheerful state of mind on the return trip. . . . Instead of staying at home and hammering away at the writing game, he had irresponsibly cut loose and gone off to the Klondike. It had been an exciting year, but a wasted one, no doubt about that. He would salvage what he could of it in short stories and articles. . . .

MINING THE KLONDIKE GOLD

It was during the quiet winter [of 1902/3] that he began, and finished in one month, the book which established his reputation internationally as a literary artist. The years of study and striving bore fruit at last in *The Call of the Wild*, of all his books the one conceived and executed with the least deliberation. He started out to write a short story, "a companion to my other dog story, 'Batard,'" he told Anna Strunsky, and even when it grew to more than thirty thousand words he still believed that he was writing merely the experiences of a dog in the Klondike. After the tale was published and reviewers and friends alike pounced enthusiastically on the human allegory inherent in the dog's life-and-death struggle to adapt himself to a hostile environment, he reread his book with astonishment. "I plead guilty," he admitted, "but I was unconscious of it at the time. I did not mean to do it."

Neither then nor later, however, did he seek to understand what had impelled him to write such a book at this time. Its warm reception, assuring him thenceforth the long-coveted status of a popular and highly paid author, destroyed whatever curiosity he may have felt concerning his own motives and perspectives. As far as he was concerned this bestseller was a purely fortuitous piece of work, a lucky shot in the dark that had unexpectedly found its mark. And again he congratulated himself on having joined the gold rush and amassed this fortune in story material. . . .

In *The Call of the Wild* he fled from the unbearable reality of the struggle for existence in capitalist civilization as he had witnessed it in the London [England] slums to a world of his own devising, a clean, beautiful, primitive world in which, he convinced himself, the fit, be they man or beast, could and would survive. At the same time, forgetting his revolutionary principles, he affirmed his belief in adaptation as the sole means of survival.

There was always the man in the red sweater who wielded a club, he argued, and there were the fangs of one's fellows ready to rend and destroy. So he enunciated "the law of club and fang": adapt yourself to the club so that in learning to conform you may be beaten but not broken; learn every trick and device in using your own fangs before your fellows spring upon you and pull you down; and do all this so that in the end you may engineer your escape from both club and fang and be your own master and the master of others.

Such good fiction all this made! Never had Jack so thoroughly enjoyed writing, never had he written so well. The teeming slums, the filth, the suffering of people doomed to go down in unequal combat vanished as he re-created the primitive Northland that he loved and wrote on that most satisfying of all themes—success. Although he did not realize it, the story of Buck's triumph was the story of his own fierce struggle to rise from poverty and squalor to a position of growing distinction and security, the story of all strong people who use the cunning of their minds and the strength of their bodies to adapt themselves to a difficult environment and win through to live, while the weak surrender and die. . . .

Because his readers, seeking refuge as eagerly as he from the complexities and defeats of modern life, clamored for more tales of victories on the frontier, further progress on this route to popularity became doubly attractive. When in a few years his interest in the revolutionary movement had flared up for the last time and died he would turn deliberately in the direction that was so pleasant to travel and paid so well. For a long time, measuring his progress by the money he earned, he was able to deceive himself that this apparently triumphant march, whose gaudy banners and strident bugles were greeted on every side with wild applause, was not a retreat. When he realized the truth it was too late.

But banners, trumpets, applause and disillusionment were as yet in the unguessed future when early in 1903 he finished the manuscript of *The Call of the Wild* and sent it off. . . .

The Call of the Wild brought to an end the comparison by well-meaning critics of Jack London's work with that of other writers. "As fine as Kipling," many had written of his first books. "He has only to go on to take the place perhaps of Stephen Crane," said others. Even Fred Lewis Pattee, revising his *History of American Literature* in 1902, had written in a footnote: "Jack London, who with a few stirring tales had made himself the Bret Harte of the Alaskan gold fields." Now Jack London stood on his own feet as an American writer, daring, forceful and original.

London's Struggle to Gain Recognition as a Writer

Jonathan Auerbach

Jonathan Auerbach notes that critics have neglected the importance of the work Buck is called upon to perform: carrying "urgent" mail. Auerbach finds parallels between Buck's travails as he tries to "get the word out" and London's need to make a name for himself as a writer. Auerbach has published *Male Call: Becoming Jack London* as well as *The Romance of Failure: First-Person Fictions of Poe, Hawthorne, and James.*

Written at a crucial juncture in London's career, just as his apprenticeship work in magazines was beginning to attract a wider national audience, *The Call of the Wild* dramatizes London's own struggle to gain recognition as a writer. Reading the dog Buck's "calling" as a mail carrier in the light of his author's aspirations, . . . I will be suggesting that London is interested in how writing gets published, how the artist/dog makes a name for himself once letters are circulated and delivered in the wild. . . .

THE VALUE AND DIGNITY OF LABOR

Learning his many "lessons" (12, 15, 18),[1] knowing his proper place, disciplining his body, and struggling for approval, Buck fulfills a higher calling. This calling has less to do with the wild than with the dignity of labor. *The Call of the Wild* thus strictly follows the dictates of the bildungsroman[2] plot in that the transformation of nature by work

---

1. Jack London, *The Call of the Wild*, in *Novels and Stories* (New York: Library of America, 1982). Subsequent page citations are from this edition. 2. bildungsroman: a novel dealing with the education and development of its protagonist.

Reprinted from Jonathan Auerbach, "Congested Mails: Buck and Jack's Call," *American Literature*, vol. 67, no. 1, March 1995. Copyright © 1995 by Duke University Press. Reprinted with permission.

leads to self-transformation, leads up from slavery to freedom. For Buck and Jack, work becomes the source of identity, the means to make a name for themselves. . . .

Initially valued strictly for his potential for work (size, strength, and ferocity), Buck's "worth" is measured in human terms by money in the marketplace (as in many slave narratives) and by other means of rational calculation: "'One in ten t'ousand,'" his new owner Perrault "comment[s] mentally" (13) during the moment of exchange.

Once Buck enters into social relations with his fellow sledmates—also the precise moment he enters into work—his "worth" takes on a new meaning. As London introduces his crew of dogs, he gives them each a distinct personality—introspective, appeasing, fair, wise, lazy, and so on—largely in relation to how Buck values them and how they value Buck. More to the point, perhaps, is how intimately these evaluations become linked to Buck's "calling," his learning to pull the sled with his mates. The ability of Sol-leks, for example, to "command respect" is limited by his lack of "apparent ambition," until Buck later sees him at work with his partner Dave and "learns" to value their "even more vital ambition" (17). Like the two "new kind of men" (13) driving them, Dave and Sol-leks on the job suddenly become "new dogs, utterly transformed by the harness. All passiveness and unconcern had dropped from them. . . . The toil of the traces seemed the supreme expression of their being, and all that they lived for and the only thing in which they took delight" (19). . . .

In an interesting footnote to his influential reading of Hegel, Alexandre Kojève remarks that animals do have "techniques" (a spider's web), but that for the world to change "essentially" and become "human," work must realize a "project" or, as he says a bit later, be activated by an "idea."[3] Through a regimen of service and self-discipline, Buck's "idea" embodied in work is to become the leader of the pack by conquering "the disciplining" (17) Spitz, his rival for mastery. Once he defeats Spitz in this "war" (29) and gains from both dogs and humans the recognition and respect for which he has struggled, then what is there left for him to do? Since Buck is part of Jack's plot, since London in

3. Alexandre Kojève, *Introduction to the Reading of Hegel* (Ithaca: Cornell Univ. Press, 1980), 52, 64.

the act of narrating is himself working *for* Buck, we are able to see glimpses of a larger project informing the labor of narration. That idea or ambition is writing itself. . . .

The most important link between Buck and writing concerns his work itself, his toiling in the traces to deliver letters. It is quite extraordinary, though hardly ever noticed by critics, that in a tale ostensibly devoted to representing the howling blank frozen white wilderness of the Yukon both men and dogs serve a noble civilizing function, bringing mail to the remotest outposts of progress, "carrying word from the world" (40). Even more pointedly, these "new men," François and Perrault, act as official agents of the state, "couriers" carrying various "government" (Canadian) "despatches" (16, 19). It is the very "important" (19) and "urgent" (32) nature of these dispatches, moreover, which accounts for the urgency of London's own labor as writer, the need to get his message out, be recognized by others for his work, and make a name for himself. As in the case of Poe's purloined letter, we never see the contents of these important dispatches, for London's emphasis falls on the delivery of mail, how writing gets circulated, distributed, and published after it is initially composed. Toiling in the traces that leave their own marks on the white landscape, both Buck and Jack fulfill their calling. . . .

THE IMPORTANCE OF MAKING A NAME

London holds very traditional assumptions about work and writing; however, I will be making a case for London's modernity by suggesting how he understands that an author's circulated name can ultimately carry more weight than the production of marks themselves.

Working like a dog finally is not enough, then, and by implication neither is writing like one. Once Buck vanquishes Spitz to achieve his highest ambition as top dog, he is soon after sold (by "official orders," 40) to a new (nameless) master, also a mailman but not apparently a government courier. London's plotting here begins to grow less urgent. The disenchanting of work actually begins shortly before Buck becomes leader of the pack. In a long, self-conscious, overheated passage celebrating "that nameless, incomprehensible pride of the trail and trace" (30), London conflates Buck's "desire for mastery" (30) over Spitz with the pride that all these dogs take "in the toil to the last gasp," the "ordained order that dogs should work" (31). But for Buck to gain supremacy over the pack, he must *disrupt* work, must break down "discipline" (32) to "destroy the solidarity of the team" (32). Describing this "challenging [of Spitz's] authority" (32) in terms of an "open mutiny" (30) or "revolt" (32), London points to a gratification beyond work: "He [Buck] worked faithfully in the harness, for the toil had become a delight to him; yet it was a greater delight slyly to precipitate a fight amongst his mates and tangle the traces" (33). It is surely no coincidence that in the very next paragraph London allows Buck and his fellows to go off chasing that wild rabbit. Working gives way to hunting, an activity more akin to play or sport that celebrates blood lust (desire) more than eating for survival (need).

While London does his best to offer the spirit of defiance as a means of transcendence that surpasses discipline and servitude, . . . the problem seems rather more mundane: sheer disgust and exhaustion with work itself. With Buck now at the lead, London suddenly remarks that "it was a monotonous life, operating with machine-like regularity. One day was very like another" (40). Pages later his last desperate effort to restore the nobility of work has precisely the opposite effect. In London's most extended treatment of another dog, something goes "wrong" with that wonderful worker Dave, who becomes "sick unto death" (43), suffering from a mysterious "inward hurt" (44) that would not go away despite his overwhelming "pride of trace and trail" (43). London settles this existential crisis as best he can, celebrating in reverent tones the fact that "a dog could break its heart through being denied the work that killed it" (44), and then finally putting Dave out of his misery with a pistol shot whose meaning Buck "knew" (44). . . .

Speaking for Buck, why should Jack in the end also find that "his heart was not in the work" (50), even as this "heart" can still remain "unbreakable" (54)? A significant clue to the answer can be found in a curious little essay entitled "How I Became a Socialist" that London first published in March 1903, just as he was negotiating the book publication rights to *The Call of the Wild.*[4] The most productive and important year of his life, 1903 also saw, among other personal events,

4. Jack London, "How I Became a Socialist," *Novels and Social Writings* (New York: Library of America, 1982), 1117–20.

the publication of London's book *The People of the Abyss*, an account of his journalistic foray the previous summer into the East End of London, where he poignantly charted the conditions of the British underclass.[5] In both essay and book London's central metaphor for this underclass is an abyss or bottomless pit; what he makes clear in his essay is that "socialism" primarily serves simply to keep him from falling into such a pit. London begins autobiographically by remarking that as a young "MAN" he used to be "one of Nietzsche's *blond beasts*," "one of Nature's strong-armed noblemen" who proudly believed that "the dignity of labor was . . . the most impressive thing in the world." Associating such "orthodox bourgeois ethics" with "rampant individualism," he claims that this "joyous individualism" was "hammered out" of him as soon as he began to come in close contact with "what sociologists love to call the 'submerged tenth'"— the underclass that industrial capitalism uses up and discards. Conveniently forgetting his own (illegitimate) birth *in* the pit of the working-class, London ends his little story with an italicized vow strange enough to merit quoting in full: *"All my days I have worked hard with my body, and according to the number of days I have worked, by just that much am I nearer the bottom of the Pit. I shall climb out of the Pit, but not by the muscles of my body shall I climb out. I shall do no more hard work, and may God strike me dead if I do another day's hard work with my body more than I absolutely have to do"* (1119). This oath is remarkable for at least three reasons. First, in disavowing his own beginnings in the pit, London "confesses" that he is primarily motivated by the "terror" of joining the underclass. He expresses absolutely no solidarity, the working-class consciousness that Marx and Engels saw as necessary for revolution. Second, given his terror of the pit, work itself becomes terrifying; the goal is not to struggle to make work less alienating and thereby rehumanize it, but merely to "run away" and escape it altogether. Third, and perhaps most remarkable, London simply

5. London started writing *The Call of the Wild* sometime during December 1902 and was finished by the middle of January 1903; the novel was serialized the following summer (beginning June 1903) in *The Saturday Evening Post*. In addition to writing the novel and the essay on socialism and preparing *The People of the Abyss* for publication the following fall, London during this remarkably productive period also published the novel *The Kempton-Wace Letters* (published anonymously, co-authored by Anna Strunsky), bought the sloop *Spray* to sail around the San Francisco Bay, began writing *The Sea Wolf* (virtually completed by the end of the year), separated from his wife and children, and fell in love with his future wife, Charmian Kittredge.

equates manual labor with "hard work." I take "hard" here also to mean "difficult," so that he is by implication suggesting that brain work would somehow necessarily be easy. . . .

London's essay might have been more accurately titled "How I Became a Successful Author," for it carries enormous implications for my previous discussion of the presence of writing throughout *The Call of the Wild*. Earlier I emphasized the physicality of writing for both Buck and Jack: hauling the heavy letters inch by inch through a blank white wilderness. Writing's materiality thus renders nature immaterial. But London's distinction between hard work and easy work suggests a second, more abstract notion of writing in which the author controls and manages the deployment of letters but does not actually carry them himself. In the scene of writing that informs the narration up to this point, London is both slave, figured as Buck toiling in the traces, and *simultaneously* figured as master, the plotter who directs the course of the sled and the beasts he uses (buys and sells) to pull it. The writing master thus hopes to gain some control within a potentially degrading capitalist market. But once hard work is fundamentally called into question, starting with the death of the dog Dave, how can letters be moved at all? That is, how can writing be strictly easy? Commenting on Hegel, Kojève notes that the bourgeois worker under capitalism has no master but nonetheless freely accepts his enslavement by the idea of private property, of capital itself.[6] London turns this fear on its head by imagining "socialism" as a state of mastery without slavery, without any hard work, so that the writer is now free to roam in search of "what manner of thing" he has suddenly become. In the end London is left looking for a kind of easy work to replace the hard work that he has given up. . . .

MASTERS—GOOD OR BAD—DO NOT DELIVER LETTERS

What remains for London then, before letting go of his plot, letting humans "pass out of Buck's life for good" (40), is to comment on the writing of the story itself through a series of

---

6. Kojève, *Introduction to the Reading of Hegel*, 65. Basing class distinctions on the difference between mental and manual labor, London uncharacteristically falls prey to a vulgar Marxism, an argument all the more surprising since his essay was published by the prominent socialist editor John Spargo, who in other contexts criticized such confused and unscientific thinking. See Daniel T. Rodgers, *The Work Ethic in Industrial America, 1850–1920* (Chicago: Univ. of Chicago Press, 1978), 219–20, 229. Presumably securing London's famous name for the socialist cause was more important than the depth of his analysis.

cautionary tales with interesting consequences. Instead of development or reversion we get a kind of stasis or holding pattern, as London presents a pair of moral lessons about bad masters and good masters. . . .

First, the bad masters, an unlikely trio of husband, wife, and wife's brother. They appear on the scene immediately after London alludes to "congested mail" (46)—a striking homonym punning on the impasse in his plot and the thwarting of Buck's manhood. New "official orders" (46), from nowhere, suddenly demand the sale of the dogs, who are said to "count for little against dollars" (46). Up to this juncture in the narrative, Buck's continuity of identity depends on carrying letters, but Charles, Mercedes, and Hal are not couriers with urgent dispatches. What they are doing venturing through the North, in fact, remains to the end a "mystery of things that passes understanding" (46)—a New Testament echo (*Philippians* 4:7) that seems to refer as much to London's uncertainty about their motives as to Buck's uncertainty, just as the subsequent paragraph's narrative commentary—"a nice family party"—seems to capture Buck's ironic disgust as well as London's.

Here then is Buck and Jack's worst "nightmare" (53), toil without writing, toil without project, toil without meaning. . . . Confronted with an alien environment, the overcivilized family registers chaos, whereas the state of wildness clearly depends on strict regimentation, possible only through regulated work. Given the absence of such service, at once ennobling and enabling, nature can be represented only by negation: what it is not. The two men unwisely overburden the dogs, the family quarrels, Mercedes gives in to "the chaotic abandonment of hysteria" (57), and all three finally and foolishly fall through thin ice, taking with them all their dogs, except for the presciently stubborn Buck. A kind of providential punishment for their poor mastery, the "yawning hole" (58) that they leave in their downward plunge serves brilliantly to literalize London's fable of negative transcendence. Hal and Charles and Mercedes have truly become the people of the abyss.[7]

Once the bad masters drop out of the picture, we might

7. Earlier in the narrative Spitz falls through the ice, leaving Buck on the slippery edge, straining in a panic with Dave and François to pull Spitz back and thereby save themselves, since they are all linked to the sled by the traces (27–28). The writing of these two fictional passages about the abyss is clearly informed by London's terror of falling into the social Pit.

expect Buck to respond immediately to the call of the wild. But before he can be free of all encumbrance he owes a debt of gratitude to his savior, John Thornton, a debt he will pay back in spectacular fashion. Entitled "For the Love of a Man," the John Thornton chapter seems totally out of place, contributing to neither Buck's working education nor his instinctual regression. . . .

A vulnerable victim finally unable to defend himself in the wilderness, Thornton is anything but lord and master by the time he meets his fate.

Thornton's "calling" as a worker follows a similar trajectory. Like the previous bad masters, this good one does not deliver letters. Nor does he do much of anything else. A wounded god, he lazily waits, as Buck does, to heal himself. Love of course is the means of healing for both, but this mutual passion soon begins to resemble suspiciously a curious kind of work whereby Buck must prove himself all over again. Their love turns into a series of perverse tests (edited from the story's first serialized version); while defending his master against a legendary desperado and then saving his life (tests #2 and #3) can be explained in terms of Buck's gratitude, a payback, how do we explain Thornton's command that Buck jump off a cliff (test #1)? Fortunately not carried out, this "experiment," which Thornton calls "splendid" and "terrible" (63), may strike the reader as not simply "thoughtless" (63), but downright sadistic. . . .

Perhaps even stranger is Buck's final test (#4), yet another "heroic" "exploit" (66) that explicitly takes the place of work. Boasting like a proud lover about the prowess of a mate, Thornton borrows money to bet heavily on Buck's ability to haul a heavy sled against a famous "Bonanza King" (67). Here the hard work of Buck as sled dog delivering letters is mocked as a kind of "free play" (69), especially when Thornton actually wins the bet, which is made for hard cold cash ($1600), rationally calculated, not for honor or dignity. By means of an empty gesture (the sled goes nowhere and is filled with dummy weight), Buck's worth is converted into market speculation. We have come full circle, since London's plot is initially triggered by betting as well: recall that Buck is sold in the first place to pay off the lottery debts of the Mexican gardener whose "faith in a [gambling] system . . . made his damnation certain" (7). For both Manuel and Thornton, Buck equals bucks.

TRADING ON HIS NAME

"When Buck earned sixteen hundred dollars in five minutes for John Thornton, he made it possible for his master to pay off certain debts and to journey with his partners into the East after a fabled lost mine, the history of which was as old as the history of the country" (71). So begins the final chapter of the novel. Given the narrative's prior emphasis on work, the devastating irony of that term "earned" is a bit troubling, as is the perfunctory nature of the rest of the rambling sentence, as if Jack simply wanted to get his story over and done with, swiftly make his *own* Big Buck, and go home to enjoy the fruits of his labor now that those "certain debts" have been discharged, thanks to Buck's five minutes of love.

Here the autobiographical and vocational dimensions of the narrative become most apparent, for John Thornton clearly doubles for John "Jack/Buck" London, as the recent excellent edition of London's letters helps us to see. Linked by London's obsessive concern with the material conditions of his craft, the writer's life and fiction tend to merge. The $1600 that Thornton wins by gambling on Buck, for example, almost matches the $1800 that London sought (and got) as an advance from his book publisher, Macmillan Company. In an extraordinary pair of letters to his editor George Brett (dated 21 Nov. and 11 Dec. 1902), London lays out an absurdly ambitious scheme to write six books in *one* year, plans filled with word counts, dollar amounts, debts, profits, market values, financial risk, and production timetables—the stuff of rationalized capitalism. London at this time (like Thornton) enjoyed "doing credit on a larger and Napoleonic scale" (letter to Cloudesley Johns, 27 Jan. 1903), in effect trading on the promise of his name.[8]

Yet despite London's heavy investment in the writer's market, the heroic deeds that Buck has performed for his master suggest another sort of economy operating in the end, an economy that depends less on Buck's work as a mail carrier and more on the spreading of his "reputation" and "name . . . through every camp in Alaska" (64). That is, the sign that Buck finally produces for himself is not the mark of writing but the mark of fame—a difference that entails a

8. Like Thornton, London was wounded, maimed during the writing of *The Call of the Wild* in a manner almost too good to be true: "A heavy box of books fell on me, striking me in a vital place" (letter to Anna Strunsky dated 20 January 1903). Here the hazards of a career in letters take on a physical dimension. See *The Letters of Jack London*, ed. Earle Labor, Robert C. Leitz III, and I. Milo Shepard (Stanford: Stanford Univ. Press, 1988), Vol. 1.

shift in the narration from work to adventure. Heroism suddenly leads to a "wander[ing]" (72) search for that "fabled lost mine"; although the Lost Cabin remains a mystery, Thornton's fabulous get-rich-quick scheme of course succeeds; London briefly narrates how "like giants they toiled, days flashing on the heels of days like dreams as they heaped the treasure up" (73), while "there was nothing for the dogs to do" (73). This self-conscious modulation into legendary fame and fortune looks forward to Buck's eventual apotheosis as immortal "Ghost Dog" (85), a kind of concluding emblem for London's career aspirations as a writer.

If this novel is an allegory at all, it should be read as an uncanny anticipation of the course of London's professional "calling," his great popularity—starting with the publication of *The Call of the Wild*!—as well as his subsequent struggles to maintain and manage his success in the literary marketplace. Striking it rich, London's revenge on his public is not to stop writing, as Buck stops working; instead London becomes driven, drives himself, to write more, to write about himself, about his own fame, over and over again until he eventually breaks down. In this respect his fate as a writer closely resembles the fate of the workaholic dog Dave, whose chronic "inward hurt"—"something wrong inside" (43) that cannot be fixed—ultimately kills him. Imagining the career of Buck, London traces a more satisfying path. As totemic leader of the (wolf) pack, Buck is obliged only to "muse" (86) dutifully at the final resting place of his beloved master, nature's own altar of the dead, sometimes bringing his wolf companions along with him. In this way we are reminded that from start to finish, Buck has never lost touch with civilization. . . .

London's progressive disenchantment with work in the story registers the growing fear felt by many turn-of-the-century American men that the market, increasingly abstract and rationalized, could no longer offer the grounds to define manhood, particularly in terms of those ideals of self-reliance, diligence, and mastery at the heart of nineteenth-century liberal individualism.[9] Once the workplace diminishes in significance in the new century, masculinity

9. There are numerous historical analyses of this crisis. See, for example, Joe L. Dubbert, "Progressivism and the Masculinity Crisis," in *The American Man*, ed. Elizabeth H. Pleck and Joseph H. Pleck (Englewood Cliffs, N.J.: Prentice-Hall, 1980), 303–20; T.J. Jackson Lears, *No Place of Grace: Antimodernism and the Transformation of American Culture, 1880–1920* (New York: Pantheon, 1981); and E. Anthony Rotundo, *American Manhood* (New York: Basic Books, 1993), chapters 10 and 11.

threatens to become primarily a performance or pose displayed for its own sake, like the theatrical shows of passion which characterize the Thornton-Buck relation ("as you love me, Buck"), and the dog-hero's equally melodramatic final conquests of bull moose, Yeehats, and wolf pack (just prior to which Buck is said to stand "motionless like a statue" [84]). Buck's toil as a letter carrier gains him respect and recognition, but his intense killing ultimately grants him the iconographic status of Ghost Dog, an awe-inspiring totem far more powerful and lasting than civilized man's paler version, fame.

Seeking to test manhood in noneconomic arenas (the wilderness, war, sports), turn-of-the-century Americans such as Teddy Roosevelt struggled to combat a mounting spiritual crisis in masculinity by trying to naturalize dominance. In one of his earlier excursions into literary criticism, an 1892 review of Kipling and other writers praising war, Roosevelt remarks that "every man who has in him any real power of joy in battle knows that he feels it when the wolf begins to rise in his heart." [10] London's own wolfish quest for power is a bit more subtle than Roosevelt's. . . . Taking Roosevelt's glib metaphor literally, London in his naturalist masterpiece imagines himself becoming—through captivity, delivering letters, and ritual slaying—the very male-creature Roosevelt can only superficially conceive of as a man in wolf's clothing. In contrast to TR's imposed metaphoric pretense, Buck under London's direction does work as a highly charged cultural carrier. For this reason *The Call of the Wild* continues to merit our attention. Simultaneously on extravagant display and buried deep, like a bone, within his animal-hero, Jack London's mail manages to affirm his own public calling—to make his bold mark for all to admire.

---

10. Theodore Roosevelt, "A Colonial Survival," in *The Works of Theodore Roosevelt* (New York: Scribner's, 1926), 12:306.

CHAPTER 4

The Novel as Literature

READINGS ON
THE CALL OF THE WILD

A Prose Poem That Has Become a World Classic

Earle Labor

Although some critics have dismissed London as a hack writer of violent dog books, the author's continued popularity after many decades suggests that academics should take another look at his work, writes Earle Labor. *The Call of the Wild* may be entertaining, but it is nonetheless an epic treatment, in prose poem form, of the myth of the hero, and should be regarded among the classics of literature. Labor, who teaches at Centenary College in Louisiana, is the author of a full-length study, *Jack London.*

In 1936, twenty years after Jack London's death, critic Arthur Hobson Quinn wrote this premature literary epitaph: "It is almost certain that his vogue is passing, for there is something impermanent in the very nature of the literature of violence." That much of the world's great literature, from Sophocles through Shakespeare to Melville, was a "literature of violence" had apparently slipped Professor Quinn's mind. Scholars of the succeeding generation nevertheless mistook his hasty judgment—insofar as it concerned the author of *The Call of the Wild*—for fact, relegating London's work—along with Robert Service's poetry, *Boys' Life*, and their merit-badge sashes—to the moldering heap of juvenile ephemerae. Among the literati Jack London became dimly remembered as a talented hack who had written some blood-and-guts stories about the supermen and superdogs of the Far North; and his name was discreetly expunged from the college-level anthologies and the critical surveys of important American writers. He might have been forgotten entirely, except for two embarrassing reminders: his works continued to sell, and a handful of sensible men ignored the obituary published by Quinn.

Excerpted from "Introduction," by Earle Labor, from *Great Short Works of Jack London* (ed. Earle Labor, NY: Harper & Row, 1965). Copyright © 1965, 1970 by Harper & Row, Publishers, Inc. Reprinted by permission of HarperCollins Publishers, Inc.

A REVIVAL OF CRITICAL INTEREST

Mere popularity is of course no gauge of literary merit, but a writer whose works have been translated into forty languages and whose popular appeal lasts beyond a half-century after his death cannot easily be dismissed as a has-been. The passing of London's vogue is indeed a curious one. The current issue of *Paperbound Books in Print* lists more than a dozen Jack London titles; the Macmillan Company continues to sell several hardbound titles and has hinted that additional volumes will soon be re-issued; London remains the most widely read American author in Europe; the Bodley Head Press in England has now published a standard edition that places his works alongside those of Ford Madox Ford and Scott Fitzgerald as significant twentieth-century authors; an upper-division course devoted to London has been inaugurated in at least one major American university; graduate students continue to mine the London lode and have as yet scarcely tapped the major vein; a half-dozen important books of Londoniana have been published during the past decade; and the obvious upsurge of interest among educated readers has prompted the issuing of a Jack London newsletter from the University of Southern Illinois. All visible signs point, in fact, not to a wake but to a major revival.

Considerable credit for the stimulation of interest among scholars is due to the work of a few men who refused to endorse the consignment of London's fiction to the dead-letter category. During the 1950s Sam Baskett, Maxwell Geismar, Gordon Mills, Franklin Walker, and C.C. Walcutt introduced London to readers of the respectable literary journals. In the 1960s the tempo of critical interest was accelerated through contributions by Clell Peterson, Alfred Shivers, and Hensley Woodbridge. And throughout these past two decades the remarkably versatile King Hendricks of Utah State University —philologist, librarian, administrator, NCAA official, and teacher—managed not only to publish several important monographs and articles on Jack London but also to sort out four hundred of the most significant items from the thousands of letters London wrote during his lifetime. The publication in 1965 of *Letters from Jack London,* edited by Hendricks and Irving Shepard (executor of the London estate), provided a crucial momentum to the revival: for the first time since London's death, critics had ready access to the heart of his private correspondence, including his statements on the craft of fiction. The fiftieth anniversary of London's death, 1966, was the *annus mirabilis*. Two books, years in the making, were published: the monumental Jack London bibliography, compiled by Woodbridge, George Tweney, and John London, with the help of more than a score of scholars from abroad; and Franklin Walker's invaluable work on London and the Klondike. *The American Book Collector* devoted an entire issue to London. And the Jack London Commemorative Meeting and Exhibition in Seattle was distinguished by the reading of tributes international in authorship.

Notwithstanding the salutary results that have been wrought by this dedicated coterie of London scholars, the primary credit for his durability is due to the quality of the literary achievement itself. No other modern writer has so successfully captivated the imaginations of readers of all ages among all peoples. The explanation for this universal appeal may be found in London's singular vitality: the "love of life" is a consistent theme in his fiction, and it was the keynote to his own fabulous personal success. The Russian scholar Vil Bykov has praised London's "deep belief in man's abilities in the face of overwhelming odds" and the "life-asserting force [of] his writings," adding significantly that "Healthy people . . . understand a healthy person. They believe in man and they tend toward that which is full of life. Jack London brought to the Russian reader a world full of romanticism and vigor, and the reader came to love him."

The man and the work are, in a sense, inseparable. Born illegitimate and reared in poverty, London became a part of all that he met and a legend in his lifetime. At the age of fifteen he was the notorious "Prince of the Oyster Pirates" on San Francisco Bay. At seventeen he shipped as an able-bodied seaman aboard the *Sophie Sutherland* for Japan and the Bering Sea (a voyage subsequently fictionalized in *The Sea Wolf*). At eighteen he hoboed his way across the continent and served a term for vagrancy in the Erie County Penitentiary (experiences later recounted in *The Road*). At twenty-one he joined the Klondike Gold Rush and prospected for the richest literary bonanza in history: "It was in the Klondike I found myself," he said afterwards; "[There you] get your true perspective. I got mine."

ACHIEVEMENTS IN LIFE AND LITERATURE

By the age of twenty-four he was publishing in the *Atlantic Monthly*; at thirty, he was the most highly-publicized writer in the world. His writing career was a relatively short one: seventeen years. But during this period, from 1899 to 1916, he lectured and wrote freely for the Socialist Party, gathered first-hand material in the London slums for an important sociological treatise (*The People of the Abyss*), supported several families, worked as a war correspondent in Korea and Mexico, designed and sailed his own ship halfway around the globe, developed one of the most beautiful country estates in the world (part of which is now the Jack London State Park in the Sonoma Valley of California), pioneered in modern agriculture and livestock breeding, and became the world's first "millionaire novelist." During these years he somehow found time to answer countless letters from fans, aspiring writers, curiosity mongers, down-and-outers, and a host of personal friends. He also wrote fifty books.

His literary achievement is our main concern here, though it should be evident that what he wrote was vitally influenced by the great short life that he lived. Three biographical factors, particularly, account for London's success as a writer: (1) the poverty that instilled a driving ambition to rise in the world; (2) the life-long wanderlust that provided the rich matrix of human experience from which his fiction is drawn; and (3) the omnivorous appetite for reading that gave him philosophical substance and a sense of artistic form. Though, like Stephen Crane, he seems to have sprung into life fully armed, his early years had furnished a wealth of those materials from which great literature is woven; he imposed upon this raw stuff of life the synthesizing forces of keen sensibility and hard-earned craftsmanship. If we accept the autobiographical *Martin Eden* as a reliable account of the young writer's initiation, there is little question that London underwent the rigorous self-imposed apprenticeship common to every professional artist. His uniqueness is that, by working eighteen hours a day, he achieved in one year the sense of craft that the ordinary writer takes ten years to master. Unlike such prose theorists as Conrad and James, London wrote almost no formal statements on the craft of fiction; but his many letters of counsel to aspiring authors reveal that he understood the fundamentals of his trade. A thoroughgoing professional, he realized early in his career that "depersonalization" is the key to successful fiction. As he advised his friend Cloudesley Johns in 1900,

> PUT ALL THOSE THINGS WHICH ARE YOURS INTO THE STORIES . . . ELIMINATING YOURSELF. . . . Atmosphere stands always for the elimination of the artist, that is to say, the atmosphere is the artist. . . . Don't narrate—paint! draw! build!—CREATE! Better one thousand words which are builded, than a whole book of mediocre, spun-out, dashed-off stuff. . . . Put in life and movement—and for God's sake no creaking. Damn you! Forget you! And then the world will remember you.

London obviously knew the concept of the "objective correlative" a generation before T.S. Eliot gave the term its modern critical status.

It should therefore come as no surprise that London's first published fruits are often as good as his last. They are, in some respects, better—because fresher. Most of his best fiction is contained in his saga of the Far North, . . . [in] novels and . . . short stories that not only attest to London's craftsmanship but also represent the major themes of . . . primitivism, atavism, environmental meliorism, stoicism, and humanism. . . .

A PROSE POEM ON THE MYTH OF THE HERO

The Call of the Wild was . . . originally intended to be a short story; . . . it became an incomparable book of 32,000 words. As occasionally happens with the gifted artist, the author wrote better than he knew. During the past sixty-odd years, *The Call of the Wild* has been translated into a score of languages and has sold more than two million copies in the American hardcover edition alone. It has become a classic which some critics are willing to place on their shelves alongside *Walden, Huckleberry Finn,* and *The Great Gatsby.* Yet, ironically, London never received a penny in royalties from the sale of his masterpiece (he sold the book outright for $2,000), and he did not like it as well as *White Fang.*

Read superficially, the story of the great dog Buck's transformation from ranch pet to Ghost Dog of the Wilderness is entertaining escape literature; but to read the novel on this level is equivalent to reading *Moby Dick* as a long-winded fisherman's yarn. Escape novels do not become world classics. Strictly speaking, *The Call of the Wild* is not a novel at all, but a prose poem with underlying rhythms of epic and myth. Its central theme is the Myth of the Hero, and interwoven with this are such myth-exponents as *initiation* (or, more accurately, *de*nitiation) the *perilous journey* (a return to the life source, or "world navel," as Joseph Campbell terms it), *transformation*, and *apotheosis.* On this level Buck is no mere animal but a symbolic projection of the reader's essential mythic *self,* as described by London ". . . sounding the deeps of his nature . . . deeper than he, going back into the womb of Time [and] mastered by the sheer surging of life." *The Call of the Wild* is London's version of "the heart of darkness" which lies beneath the protective layers of civilization, society, and super ego within all men. The "uncharted vastness" penetrated by John Thornton's party near the end of the book is enveloped appropriately in the atmosphere of the dream world; it is the timeless landscape of myth. And when London writes that "Like giants they toiled, days flashing on the heels of days like dreams as they heaped the treasure up," he is obviously modulating his imagery in terms of a farther and deeper music than that of the ordinary, phenomenal world. Buck's is a world of the *un*conscious (Jung called it the "collective unconscious"), the primordial world against which modern man has erected inhibiting barriers of rationality and the social ethic but a nonetheless real world to which he would return, in dreams, to find his soul. Within this inchoate wilderness, "through the pale moonlight or glimmering borealis," flashes the Ghost Dog, symbol of libido, *élan vital,* the essential life force. And it is to this call—the faint but clear music of life's ultimate mystery—that the reader subtly responds. . . .

PHILOSOPHIC INTEGRITY AND MYTHIC FORCE

Memorable as London's Northland heroes are, they are less impressive than the setting itself. In the same way that the great white whale dominates Herman Melville's masterpiece, becoming the main character by virtue of his supernatural awesomeness, so the White Silence overshadows London's human protagonists. As he writes in "The White Silence," in *The Son of the Wolf*

> Nature has many tricks wherewith she convinces man of his finity,—the ceaseless flow of the tides, the fury of the storm, the shock of the earthquake, the long roll of heaven's artillery,—but the most tremendous, the most stupefying of all,

is the passive phase of the White Silence. All movement ceases, the sky clears, the heavens are as brass; the slightest whisper seems sacrilege, and man becomes timid, affrighted at the sound of his own voice. Sole speck of life journeying across the ghostly wastes of a dead world, he trembles at his audacity, realizes that his is a maggot's life, nothing more. Strange thoughts arise unsummoned, and the mystery of all things strives for utterance. And the fear of death, of God, of the universe, comes over him,—the hope of the Resurrection and the Life, the yearning for immortality, the vain striving of the imprisoned essence,—it is then, if ever, man walks alone with God.

In portraying this natural phenomenon, London, like Melville, seized upon the symbolic latencies of *whiteness*: the terrifying all-color of cosmic mystery "that by its indefiniteness [wrote Melville] shadows forth the heartless voids and immensities of the universe, and thus stabs us from behind with the thought of annihilation . . ."; or, in terms of myth, whiteness becomes the "archetype" for an impersonal, incomprehensible but overwhelming deity of endless contradictions. It is this symbolic presentation of landscape as deity—not beneficent but inviolable, stark, and above all, Absolute—which imparts to the Northland saga its philosophic integrity as well as its mythic force.

Whether or not Jack London was fully aware of these implications in his work is open to question. The question itself may be irrelevant in view of the admonition by D.H. Lawrence that we should never trust the teller, but trust the tale instead. Trusting London's tales, we cannot escape the realization that he possessed an exceptional mythopoeic genius, the quality that Carl Jung called "primordial vision":

> What is essential in a work of art [Jung tells us] is that it should rise far above the realm of personal life and speak from the spirit of the heart of the poet as man to the spirit and heart of mankind. . . . The secret of artistic creation and of the effectiveness of art is to be found in a return to the state of *participation mystique*—to that level of experience at which it is man who lives, and not the individual, and at which the weal or woe of the single human being does not count, but only human experience.

This artistic vitality and universality is the secret of Jack London's fictional creation and the reason that, while the material turned out by academic critics may go stale, his best work remains perennially fresh.

The Failure of an American Myth

Abraham Rothberg

Jack London failed to live up to his promise as a self-made individualist, writes Abraham Rothberg. He accepted responsibility for his successes but not for his lapses, and burned himself out by the age of forty. *The Call of the Wild*, his best work, presents his unconscious allegory about the dog-eat-dog world of humans; while the story reflects his desire to escape from the capitalist world, the escape his hero finds directly opposes his self-proclaimed socialist beliefs. Rothberg wrote his dissertation on London: *The House That Jack Built: A Study of Jack London, the Man, His Times, and His Works.*

Jack London is an American myth, a combination of personal myths he created about himself and a national myth he represented in his life and work. His continued influence for almost fifty years since his death is in great measure due to the vitality of these myths. London is the Horatio Alger myth of the poor boy who became a millionaire by pulling himself up by his own bootstraps. London is also the revolutionary myth—he signed his letters, "Yours for the Revolution"—of the rebel who wanted to pull society down by its pillars. London is the red-blooded writer and war-correspondent who "went everywhere and did everything," adopting the cloak that Hemingway would later throw over his own literary shoulders. London is the alcoholic who destroyed his own talent and who was dead at forty, already foretelling Scott Fitzgerald's "Babylon Revisited" and *The Crack Up.* London is the artist who wanted desperately to be a success in business and failed in the same bitter way as had his contemporary, Mark Twain.

But London is more than the American myth, and fact, of the blighted career, the writer who makes a brilliant beginning and then cannot develop from there, the artist who cannot cope with America's "business is business," and the Horatio Alger success myth. Europeans have seen his life and work, and used them, to make and maintain a myth of American life and character. Europe, and the Soviet Union in particular, have made London one of their most popular and widely read American writers because they like to see him as an "American Gorky" whose view of nineteenth-century American capitalism is still a contemporary reality instead of an epoch in United States history long past and dead.

London not only showed the inherent virtues of the American character—our energy and love of action and the strenuous life, our generosity, courage, and concern for social justice—he also portrayed our most pernicious vices— our contentiousness and violence, our recklessness, our materialism, and our love of change for its own sake. Europeans and Russians tend to overlook the virtues and concentrate on London's view of our vices. This has reinforced the caricature of the American so dear to European hearts, the "simplified husky American . . . with a checkbook in one hind pocket and a revolver in the other."

Jack London was a complex man whose talent was never quite able to cope with that complexity in his work, or, for that matter, in his life. But it did succeed, through the very contradictoriness of his nature, in mirroring the conflicting forces of his time, the tumultuous America at the end of the nineteenth century known, too simply, as the Gilded Age, the Age of Horatio Alger, and the Age of the Robber Barons. If London's life and work are mythic creations, they are also realities to conjure with; they tell a very great deal not only about a tormented and talented man who burned himself out in a brief lifetime of forty years, but about the America in which London lived and worked, and whose myths he simultaneously embodied and scored.

EARLY FACTORS SHAPED PERSONALITY

Jack London was born on January 12, 1876. He was the illegitimate son of Flora Wellman and an itinerant astrologer named William Henry Chaney. Only in September of the same year, when Flora married John London, was John Chaney's name changed to the one he was to make famous: John Griffith London. His mother was a driving woman in whom the remains of the pioneer spirit had become a fly-by-night restlessness. She was constantly plunging into schemes for making a fortune overnight. Jack's stepfather, a quiet, gentle man with a love of the soil and animal breeding, was unable to cope with either her ambition or her terrible fits of temperament. As a result she drove him into a series of business fiascos all over the San Francisco Bay area—Alameda, San Mateo, Livermore, Emeryville, and Oakland—desperately striving to improve their condition and inevitably making it worse. This pattern of failure and flight was to scar London permanently.

Not only was Flora temperamentally unsuited for motherhood, but hard work, spiritualist meetings and business scheming left her little time or energy for her first-born. Possibly her resentment of Chaney and the circumstances of Jack's birth also tainted her love for the boy. Added to the precarious place he held in his mother's affections was the knowledge of his illegitimacy, of which Jack was soon to become aware. This knowledge weighed heavily on him and was one of the most important factors in shaping his personality.

In his reactions to his parents and to the conditions of his childhood can be seen some of the origins of London's dilemmas and concerns. In Flora, the boy could see and respect driving and overbearing individualism, the first impulse toward adopting the Nietzschean superman; in his sympathy for the kindly and beaten John London lay the roots of his concern for the people and socialism. For many years a marginal middle-class family, in Oakland the Londons were finally and definitely forced into the working class by a combination of John London's aging and illness, Flora's continued financial irresponsibility, and the economic conditions of the late 1880's. As Flora's grandiose schemes were to instance London's later wild flyers in business, so John London's love of farming and animal husbandry was instilled in the boy. As a man, Jack London was to make them his chief preoccupations on his Valley of the Moon Ranch.

The contrast between their working-class conditions and Flora's middle-class values intensified Jack's own Horatio Alger aspirations; in spite of his position in the economic cellar of society, London was determined to succeed. In this urge to escape from the working class lay another anchor for

London's individualism; in his actual position in the working class was the foundation for his sympathy for the masses
and for socialism. The way to climb the social ladder was, of
course, through business, enterprise and individualism; the
way to eliminate the cellar of society was through revolutionary socialism.

CREATING A PERSONAL MYTH

London's shame and guilt about his poverty and illegitimacy
worked with these conflicting impulses and led him to try to
convert his liabilities into assets. And so he created the
myths with which he was gradually to wrap his life and
eventually to make into his shroud. Jack exaggerated and
distorted the facts of his early struggles into a background of
overwhelming poverty. Thus inflated, the circumstances
made London appear all the more superior an individual for
having overcome them; in so doing he had tempered his
steel and proved his mettle. And, under the influence of his
mother's racist bias, he could also boast that he was a blond-
beast Anglo-Saxon (which he was not), thus substituting
pride of racial lineage for the shame of illegitimacy.

For London, life's choices were swiftly polarized: he could
be either beast of prey or beast of burden; he could either escape from civilization to its more primitive outer edges, or involve himself in society and succeed in its terms. In "The
Tramp," an essay published many years later, London as-
tutely pointed out that the tramp is either a discouraged
worker or a discouraged criminal—or both, delineating the
alternatives London had seen for himself, felt and personally
explored. Desperate to escape from the social pit, filled with
rebellious aggressiveness and self-destruction, London alter-
nated between trying to be a "work beast" or a beast of prey,
between flight from the society and aggression against it.

From a back-breaking job as a work beast in a cannery,
London switched to being a "burglar in a boat," or an oyster
pirate; then he turned on the oyster pirates by joining the
state Fish Patrol which policed them. At 17, London signed
on a ship as an able-bodied seaman and fled to the sealing
grounds off Japan, only to find when he returned home that
the depression of 1893 forced him back to being a work
beast in a jute mill, and then a coal-heaver in a power plant.
In revolt and out of revulsion, London became a tramp and
hit the road. After joining "Kelly's Army," the Western

branch of Jacob Coxey's army of unemployed who were then marching on Washington to protest economic conditions, Jack not only had become part of a mass-social protest group, but also lived off the countryside begging from the farmers. In addition, with a group of cronies, he also tried to get the cream of the provisions that sympathetic farmers donated by going ahead of the Army and stealing it. After leaving the Army and hoboing around the country, London was finally imprisoned for vagrancy in the Erie County Penitentiary near Niagara Falls, New York.

Throughout, however, facts were always interwoven with fantasy, and it remains impossible to disentangle the two. Whether London was actually an oyster pirate or worked for the Fish Patrol is open to question, as are the myths of his physical and alcoholic prowess, his attempts at suicide, and his sailor-in-port splurging and generosity. But if London warped facts into myths, he lived the myths in turn, and made them facts to feed new myths.

The events of 1894 were crucial in London's life. The penitentiary, the road and Kelly's Army reinforced the lessons of his early experiences and their philosophy of dog-eat-dog and devil-take-the-hindmost. His hostility for and rebellion against society increased because of the cruelties and injustices he had seen and endured. London had been frightened so badly that he felt he needed a new way to deal with it all. Out of that fright, developed an interest in socialism which became superimposed on his assertive individualism. The two contrary impulses were to co-exist for the rest of his life. In addition, so terrifying had those experiences been that London decided to chance his own style of life. He had decided that brawn wore out too quickly and was paid for too cheaply; if one wanted out of the social pit, one had to sell brain power: it lasted longer and paid better.

As a result, London decided to return home to become a "brain merchant.". . .

SUCCESS WITHOUT SATISFACTION

By 1902, the year his first novel, *A Daughter of the Snows*, was published, he was married, had two children, a house, and more income than he had ever dreamed of. But satisfaction eluded him. The days of his youth haunted him with their struggle and privation, and gave rise to exaggerated pessimism, despair and self-pity. But London could not accept responsibility for anything but his successes. For his other actions, feelings and circumstances he blamed external things: books, alcohol and its "White Logic," and "the system." As his marriage began to founder, he took a journalist's assignment abroad. When the assignment fell through, and Jack found himself in London, he decided to go into the city's slums, the East End, dressed like a beached American sailor, taking with him only "certain simple criteria with which to measure the life of the underworld. That which made for more life, for physical and spiritual health was good; that which made for less life, which hurt, and dwarfed and distorted life, was bad."

What he saw in the London slums brought back memories of the Oakland slums, and of the road and the penitentiary. It frightened him with its misery and hopelessness. He was only too recently out of the abyss himself and still too uncertain about remaining out of it to be detached. The system that produced such squalor and wretchedness he hated, but the more he saw of the abyss, the more certain he became that its inhabitants could not change their circumstances. Not only did he lose much of his faith in the working classes in the East End, he lost much of his faith in civilization itself. . . .

ALLEGORY AND AUTOBIOGRAPHY

Back in California in the winter of 1903, London began the short story which was to run away from him and become a novel, *The Call of the Wild*. In it, the meaning of Buck's attempt to survive in the hostile northland was deeply influenced by what London had so recently seen in the East End. London was unaware of the book's allegorical dog-eat-dog principle in human affairs, and admitted that he was, but it and the escape motif were plainly there.

Not only was *The Call of the Wild* an allegory, it was a kind of autobiography as well. London's close identification with the wolf and the dog, in his life and in his books, is everywhere evident. He was delighted when friends called him "Wolf" or "Shaggy Wolf," he signed his letters "Wolf," had his bookmarks engraved with the picture of a big wolf-dog's face, and went so far as to call his baronial manor the "Wolf House." London was not only telling the story of Buck's life, but of his own, demonstrating the principles of success and survival he had learned. He had seen civilization—the East End, the Oakland slums, the road, and jail, and had chosen savagery—the Alaskan wilds. The reality of the capitalism he could not cope with was abandoned for a simpler, more primitive world; the complexities of human behavior were jettisoned in favor of the more fundamental behavior of dogs and wolves. And the fittest who survived there were those who employed individual strength, cunning and violence against nature, man and society, *not* those who employed socialist mass action against institutionalized injustice. Nor did they succeed by revolutionary assertion; they survived by adapting to the "law of club and fang.". . .

LONDON'S FEELINGS ABOUT HIMSELF AND SOCIETY

With his second novel, London became an important writer; *The Call of the Wild* is the most perfectly realized novel he ever wrote. Out of his fearful plunge into the London abyss and his consequent retreat in fiction to the primitive world of dogs and Alaska came an allegory of human life. A study of atavism, or reversion to type, it was also an allegory of man's conditions in the society of London's time as well as a revelation of the deepest emotions London felt about himself and that society.

The novel has three levels, the first and narrative one the story of a dog, Buck, who reverts to type, learns to survive in a wolf-like life, and eventually becomes a wolf. The second, or biographical level reveals what London himself lived and felt in climbing out of the abyss of poverty and deprivation to prestige as a writer and wealth. Buck was symbolically Jack London struggling for success and domination, learning the law of club and fang, "put into harness," and finally becoming the shaggy wolf rampant. The third level is political and philosophical, exemplifying the doctrines of social Darwinism in fictional form. The fittest survive by adaptation to the man with the club (the stronger individual) and the strength of the herd (the power of the masses). By this adaptation man or dog may be temporarily defeated but ultimately will triumph. Man or dog becomes hardened to nature physically and also hardened spiritually to greed, thievery, cunning, violence, and individualism in society and nature. Finally, when man or dog has gained sufficient strength and craft, he may prey on those weaker than himself, knowing that, as London saw it, "Mercy did not exist in the primordial life. It was misunderstood for fear, and such misunderstanding made for death. Kill or be killed, eat or be eaten, was the law."

London was not only treating animals like human beings, but treating human beings like animals, recognizing no essential difference between man and animal. In *The Call of the Wild* he equated men with dogs and wolves, and equated the harshness of the trail with the harshness of society, implying that force, savagery and cunning were equally the ways to success in both areas. London's vocabulary also carried and reinforced his meaning. Buck is "put into harness," the human phrase for working. He becomes "lead-dog," or in man's parlance, "top-dog." He is forced to meet and bow to "the man with the club," an almost cliché expression for power and authority. Buck leads the "wolf pack," to which he finally reverts, a predatory term still in use in our own day. The very fact that London deals with a "dog's life"— Humankind's frequent comment on its own condition is that "It's a dog's life."—indicates how thoroughgoing was his view.

Beneath man's veneer of civilization, London saw a prehistoric beast who fought and conquered through might and deceit, whose nature was fierce and cruel in the extreme. Scratch the veneer, and the prehistoric beast shone through, atavism took place, and man reverted to the "wolf." Buck, the civilized dog, devolves to where he not only kills but enjoys killing. London's love of violence and bloodshed is here, and elsewhere, rendered as a "wine-of-life," "strength-through-joy," emotion, and to Buck he gives it as a lust "to kill with his own teeth and wash his muzzle to the eyes in warm blood."

The only thing that keeps Buck from the wild is his love of man, just as love had held London, and just as love as well as fear holds most of mankind from the war of all against all, in spite of Hobbes' dictum that "Man is as a wolf to man." In life, however, love eventually dies or is killed, as John Thornton is killed by the Yeehats, and then Buck (and therefore man) reverts to the savagery of the wolf-pack, following the primordial call of the wild. . . .

VIOLENCE, NOT JUSTICE

The contradictions of [London's] life and work are the contradictions of the era which shaped him and his ideals. . . .

While he continued to be the novelist of frontier types and conditions, London was also supposed to be a proletarian writer. Not only did he escape to the primitive, therefore, he

simultaneously stood his native ground to express his resistance to and criticism of the new industrial society. And he
did write about working people, about industrial strife, and
about success in capitalist society. But London's working-
class writing cannot accurately be called either "proletarian" or "socialist." The revolution for him was really a pri-
mordialism in which the beast, ape and tiger in man might
be released. What interested him most in the mass was its
potential for violence. What he craved most was not the social justice which was supposed to result from the revolution, but the bloodletting of the revolutionary process itself.
What he wanted to do was to master the masters of society,
and consequently, and significantly, the socialist doctrines
he stresses most are class struggle and violent revolution.

The plight of the people and London's sympathy for them
and for it are always tinged with contempt. London depicts
the masses as ugly, rapacious, violent, and faceless, an insight into the roots of his revolutionary spirit, and a demon-
stration that it was more an outlet for his own social aggres-
sions than an ethical or philosophical conviction. This
temperamental romantic rebellion went into the individual
and collectivist approaches alike. The picture of the superman had, after all, been a fictional aggrandizement; London
was creating a compensatory myth for not having been the
success in strength, business, love, or even in writing, that
he had anticipated. Failing that, his romanticism and rebellion were channelled into participation in the power of the
mass against the system that had prevented his aggrandize-
ments. . . .

THE FAILURE OF SUCCESS

Right up to his death, Jack London was still attached, at least
verbally, to those ideals he had almost abandoned in personal and political action. He still raised a cry for justice,
sympathy, service and unselfishness in transforming society. "He, who by understanding, becomes converted to the
gospel of service . . . will serve kindness so that brutality will
perish. . . . And he who is strong will serve the weak that they
may become strong. He will devote his strength, not to the
debasement and defilement of his weaker fellows, but to the
making of opportunity for them to make themselves into
men rather than into slaves and beasts."

However wrung from the depths of a tormented and riven

soul that cry was, it was compromised by London's failure to apply its disciplines to his life and work. Ultimately, London failed in what he wanted to be and to do. The problems to which he addressed himself are, in the main, still relevant and important today, but the materials and approach with which he addressed himself to them are dated and over-simplified, too irrational and too schematically logical. As such, Jack London's failure is one more instance of the failure of success in America and, as such, is a symptom and a menace from which our own age can and should profitably learn.

The Call of the Wild Stands the Test of Time

Robert Barltrop

Because Jack London's works are not difficult to read, writes London biographer Robert Barltrop, they have often not been taken seriously as literature. Romantic fantasy may not garner the respect given to weightier genres, but London's fantasies, including *The Call of the Wild*, were both unique and ahead of their time, according to Barltrop. While he may not rank in the highest tier of literature, no one is better than he is in the field of imaginative storytelling, and his continued popularity so many decades after his death merits respect.

Jack London's books have not been taken seriously as literature. At best, he is seen as an enjoyable but unimportant writer, and his work is frequently treated with contempt. In *Intellectual America* Oscar Cargill refers to him, Upton Sinclair and Dreiser as 'witless, heavy-handed progeny' of earlier realist writers like Frank Norris. Later in the same book Cargill says there is little indication that Jack London and others of his school knew 'or cared to know' what 'the genuine primitive' was. Other critics acknowledge his popularity, but discount it on literary grounds.

Such judgements have not deterred readers of Jack London's books but often create a kind of guilt over reading them: the right to triviality is claimed, a little defiantly. However, it is not uncommon for literary criticism to forget what literature is. Most popular fiction is essentially ephemeral, having no virtue beyond meeting some need of the hour. When further merits are claimed, they have a habit of fading away when the hour has gone. There are no readers of Marie Corelli and A.S.M. Hutchinson today, and no critics urging that they should be read. But if a writer continues to give satisfaction to large numbers of people for a long enough period, he becomes entitled to a place of respect in literature. The needs he meets have been shown to be not transient. It is sixty years since Jack London died, and seventy since his major books were written. Most of them are reprinted throughout the literate world. He cannot be dismissed.

The most obviously striking thing about his work is its quantity. His first book was published in 1900. Including the seven which were published posthumously, by 1916 he had produced 50 books: an average persistently maintained of more than three a year. In addition he made outlines and notes for several more, and half-wrote *The Assassination Bureau* (it was completed by Robert L. Fish and published in 1963). Many of the books are not particularly long. The volumes of short stories are mostly about 50,000 words altogether; some other works—*The Call of the Wild, The Scarlet Plague, The Game*— are barely long enough to be considered novels. By the normal standards of fiction writing Jack's output would be represented in thirty-odd books instead of fifty. That is still a notable product of sixteen years' work. If his journalism is added, it approximates to his thousand words every day throughout those years.

Something like a third of the work does not come in for consideration from any point of view. It is doubtful if anyone today reads the South Sea stories or *Hearts of Three. The Cruise of the Dazzler* and *Tales of the Fish Patrol* are schoolboy yarns; *A Daughter of the Snows, The Abysmal Brute* and *The Little Lady of the Big House* have interest only for students of Jack London. These and a few others were produced for the market, with little to commend them other than his reputation and no claim on posterity. The three plays he wrote—*Scorn of Women, Theft* and *The Acorn Planter*—were all unsuccessful, and most people do not even know of their existence.

AHEAD OF HIS TIME

What is remarkable about the two-thirds of Jack's work on which his popularity rests is the extent to which it was ahead of the taste or the mood of his time. He achieved fame quickly as a writer of vigorous, lucid adventures in the frozen north and at sea. With this reputation as a story-teller established, nothing he wrote was likely to be rejected. Nevertheless, the fact is that the Jack London books which are the most widely read and esteemed today were all doubtful properties when they were published. *The Call of the Wild* and *The People of the Abyss* were successful against expectations. *The Iron Heel, The Road, Martin Eden* and *The Star Rover* (*The Jacket*) were received either coolly or with actual disparagement.... Yet without these he would not be famous: known perhaps as an excellent short-story writer, but without major works to his credit.

The reason for doubting whether the public in 1903 would find *The Call of the Wild* acceptable has been noted—its departure from the convention of sentimentality in animal stories. Leaving aside *The Iron Heel*, because it is a special case in every sense, something similar can be said of the other books that either did not expect or did not find favour in Jack's lifetime. *The Road* and *The Jacket* both describe prison life in horrific terms. That, indeed, is the fascination of *The Jacket*. Its historical fantasies vary from the ordinary to the wishy-washy, but the background of the punishment cell grips the reader's imagination. In the early nineteen-hundreds this was fundamentally unsuitable material. A sentimental account of a prison episode, such as Wilde's in *The Ballad of Reading Gaol*, was thought sufficiently daring as the alternative to Dickensian pictures of the wicked receiving their deserts. In showing the brutality of prisons, with more than an implication that justice was a sham anyway, Jack London was a generation in advance of his time....

TRUTH IS NOT REALISM

Jack London's themes were taken directly from his own experiences, and his treatment of them took no account of being 'nice'. Many of his stories are autobiographical, narrating incidents in his life either openly in the first person, as in *The Road* and *John Barleycorn*, or with slight disguises of names and circumstances. Not infrequently he used the names of people he had known in a way which would be unthinkable to libel-haunted English writers. Ernest Everhard is one example, though he borrowed the name alone without otherwise involving the cousin he had once met. In several other cases he used a person whole, as it were, under the person's own name. From his Klondike days there were Elam Harnish, the hero of *Burning Daylight*; Father Roubeau, the priest in *The Son of the Wolf*; and, perhaps most remarkable of all, Freda Moloof. Appearing as a good-natured whore in 'Scorn of Women', she was a dancer whom Jack had known in Dawson City; when he found her living in San Francisco, he presented her with a copy of the book.

His stories appear to be true. In matters of detail they undoubtedly were true. At times when he was challenged over authenticity he was always able to reply with the certainty of first-hand experience. In 1909 he wrote answering an article called 'The Canada Fakers' that had appeared in the journal *Canada West*. A characteristic part of his letter runs:

> You object to my use of the dog-driver's command of 'mush on'. My northland stories are practically all confined to the Klondike and to Alaska, and there the only phrase used as a command for the dogs to get up, to go on, to move, is 'mush on'. There is no discussion about this fact. There is no man who has been in Klondike or Alaska but who will affirm this statement of mine.

To a Klondike acquaintance he wrote: 'Yes, Buck was based upon your dog at Dawson and of course Judge Miller's place and Judge Bond's—even to the cement swimming tanks and the artesian well.'[1]

Yet the use of existing people and true events is not in itself realism. The fact is that Jack London's stories have their persistent appeal because, ultimately, they are not realistic at all: they are romantic fantasy. It is not just the case that they bring a world of distant excitement to town-dwellers; the world is adapted to be as the reader wants it, rather than as he would have found it. . . .

A LAND OF MANLY ADVENTURES

Nevertheless, Jack London's fantasies are not the same as the fantasies created by most popular writers. He had created them for himself. In practically everything he did in his life, romantic images obscured what things and people were really like. The failures in his personal relationships and his projects were certainly due to this; the idealisation of his experiences in his stories was not simply a selective view from a safe distance, but expectations he had taken into—and, apparently, preserved through—those experiences. One reason is that the experiences of oyster-pirating, the sea, tramping and the Klondike were all short-term, enabling him to feel a member of an exalted and glamorous brotherhood without the disenchanting effects of time. He entered and left them with mental pictures formed by his boyhood reading.

1. Letter to Marshall Bond, 17 December 1903.

His vision was the same as his readers'. Just as they envis-
aged a northland full of manly adventures and populated by
such characters as the Malemute Kid, so did he. He voiced
their feeling that it was far above the life led by the majority of
people, that it bred a higher type of man. Smoke Bellew reflects
on it:

> Alone, with no one to talk to, he thought much, and deeply, and
> simply. He was appalled by the wastage of his city years, by the
> cheapness, now, of the philosophies of schools and books, of the
> clever cynicism of the studio and editorial room, of the cant of
> the business men in their clubs. They knew neither food, nor
> sleep, nor health; nor could they possibly ever know the sting of
> real appetite, the goodly ache of fatigue, nor the rush of mad
> strong blood that bit like wine through all one's body as work
> was done.

A number of the stories represent extremes of fantasy. The
beautifully told 'The Night Born' is an example: the sort of sexual episode away from civilisation that most men daydream of
at some time.

No doubt many thousands of people in Jack's own time half-
believed they might have such adventures, given the opportunity. The legend of the frontiersmen was still potent. Jack's reputation for realism came partly from this belief, and also
because his stories had a full measure of toughness. Death is
frequent in them, usually by violence; disease, frostbite and
scurvy appear regularly, and leprosy is used in several of the
South Seas stories. In fact this is another aspect of romanticism. What is signified is the 'law of life' which Jack laid down.
It replaces explanation and makes human efforts redundant:
'this is how it is', the author is saying.

Several of the stories are built round this principle. Perhaps
the best is a boxing story, 'A Piece of Steak'. Its chief character
is a hard-up, aging fighter who is matched with a rising
younger man. His skill just fails to master the other's greater
strength and speed. As he walks home, he thinks how narrow
a thing it was and how he could have won if he had been able
to afford a piece of steak beforehand. The excellence of the
story comes from leaving it there, without expressions of sentiment: in time the same thing will happen to the younger
man. While we know it is true, there is the feeling that the
writer likes the idea of it being true—'the law' is like God, dis-
posing of man regardless of what he proposes. . . .

His best [work] is to be found in a number of short stories
which establish him as one of the masters of that form. A col-

lection of these outstanding stories would include 'The Apostate', 'The Mexican', 'Love of Life'—the ending is an irrelevance rather than a weakness, 'A Piece of Steak', 'The Night Born', and 'To Build a Fire'. There are six or seven others which are very good by any standard: 'The *Francis Spaight*', 'Under the Deck Awnings'. 'Just Meat', 'The Benefit of the Doubt'. In addition, *The Cruise of the Snark* and *The Road* are collections of episodes which can be read separately; 'Hoboes That Pass in the Night' and 'Holding Her Down' are little gems of writing which are both stimulating and informative.

The reason why these have, on the whole, been denied literary importance is their subject-matter. Whatever the quality of Jack London's stories, they are not taken seriously because their material does not reflect—indeed, it provides an escape from—life as the mass of people know it. This applies not only to the Klondike and the South Seas stories, but to those which are about boxers and tramps; equally, these represent attractive, disreputable sub-worlds of fantasy. Comparison can be made with American writers of the early part of this century—Sinclair Lewis, for example—who, with narrative ability inferior to Jack London's, won critical praise for their pictures of the known contemporary world. Since that world changes, there is no reason why London should not be recognised as a writer of high order. The place for him in literature is much on a level with Maupassant's. His view was too restricted for the place to be a topmost one, but in the field of imaginative story-telling his work cannot be bettered.

Writers are said to stand, or not to stand, 'the test of time'; certainly many books by favoured writers are tedious, two generations after their time. Almost anyone who begins a Jack London book finds himself absorbed by the progression of events and the liveliness of the style. This is the case even when the story is preposterous; there is a quality (perhaps it is the art of the story-teller) which makes heavily melodramatic incidents seem valid. . . .

DEVELOPING HIS OWN STYLE

Jack's early stories bear the marks of his study of Kipling. The narrative presents no problems, but there are self-conscious discourses in which he can be seen searching for aids to writing well. These quickly disappeared as confidence was gained, and after the first two or three books his style becomes distinctly his own. It is essentially a journalistic style, almost reporter-like when he is describing action. However, it contains another journalistic element which became the worst fault in his writing: repetition. The reiteration of phrases, from a useful device, was turned into a cheap way of obtaining emphasis. . . .

However, the writing of Jack's best years is frequently superb. It contains not only movement without reiteration, but some beautiful descriptive passages. *The Call of the Wild* has a series of haunting descriptions of the northland he had known.

> The months came and went, and back and forth they twisted through the uncharted vastness, where no men were and yet where men had been if the Lost Cabin were true. They went across divides in summer blizzards, shivered under the midnight sun on naked mountains between the timber line and the naked snows . . . In the fall of the year they penetrated a weird lake country, sad and silent, where wild-fowl had been, but where there was no life or sign of life—only the blowing of chill winds, the forming of ice in sheltered places, and the melancholy rippling of waves on lonely beaches.

These passages drew upon the notebooks he had kept and the imagery formed by his early reading. In later years he became preoccupied with finding plots and situations. He kept boxes of newspaper cuttings, and looked for themes in everything he read and saw. It has been suggested, on the basis of stories like 'Law of Life', 'Love of Life', 'To Build a Fire' and 'The Apostate', that he functioned best as a writer when dealing with individuals isolated in a given background. A wider survey provides no support for this. Rather, it appears that he was dependent on turning up or being supplied with ideas for action against backgrounds with which he was familiar. The effectiveness of the results depended on his attitude to his work—more than anything, on what was happening in his personal life.

Broadly, there are two classes of Jack London reader. His adventure stories have a huge international public; and he is a writer with a special appeal to socialists and radicals. Obviously there is a substantial overlap between these two sections, but it is by no means necessary; *The Call of the Wild* and *White Fang* are classics in Spain, where his political writings are banned. While the radical affection for him is closely connected with the legend that he was, despite his vagaries, a fighter for the underdog, its strongest roots are in the dream of a 'working-class literature'. This has existed ever since the emergence of labour movements. It has never been realised; and of the few writers who came near fulfilling it, Jack London was the only one to achieve fame. . . .

The merit of Jack London's writings about socialism and revolution is . . . 'crudity'—their vigour and simplicity. It is true that he captured a unique combination of social factors that cannot be reproduced. They included the swift, almost violent transformation of American society; the growth of an energetic but confused radical movement; the technical innovations which brought into being a popular press looking for writers who expressed the aspirations of the time. He can be identified also with a type well-known for a hundred years in Britain but transitory in America—the self-educated working man. Part of his individuality was undoubtedly due to accidents of circumstance: with greater stability in his upbringing, or had he remained at university, he would have been a better-adjusted person. In that case, it is unlikely that we should have the writer who, repudiating the description of himself as a scholar and man of letters, said:

> Before people had given me any of these titles . . . I was working in a cannery, a pickle factory, was a sailor before the mast, and spent months at a time looking for work in the ranks of the unemployed; and it is the proletarian side of my life that I revere the most, and will cling to as long as I live.[2]

2. In an address to a socialist meeting in Los Angeles in 1905.

Contradictions in *The Call of the Wild*

Charles Frey

The complex contradictory issues raised by London are one key to the lasting appeal of *The Call of the Wild*, writes essayist and literature scholar Charles Frey. Frey notes that London explores many sets of opposing values, including north vs. south, civilization vs. primordial savagery, masculinity vs. femininity, life as woe or as ecstasy, and work as fulfilling or as deadening. Raising such a host of provocative questions without providing easy answers indicates that the book is much more than escapist fantasy.

The Call of the Wild, published in 1903 when Jack London was twenty-seven and since read by world-wide millions, old and young, is easily criticized as escapist fantasy. The book's hero, the huge dog Buck, is first presented as a pampered favorite child and as a product of civilization's finest comforts, comforts swiftly made to seem paltry things. Buck lives in the "sun-kissed Santa Clara Valley," in the soft and civilizing Southland. His home offers both protection from the world (the house stands "back from the road, half hidden among the trees") and selfconscious pride of exalted place in the world. Buck carries himself in "right royal fashion." "During the four years since his puppyhood he had lived the life of a sated aristocrat; he had a fine pride in himself, was even a trifle egotistical, as country gentlemen sometimes become because of their insular situation." Buck, plainly enough, is due for a lesson. Kidnapped and taken north, he learns that he has been "an unduly civilized dog," but he soon loses "the fastidiousness which had characterized his old life." Buck adapts, as a sled dog in the Yukon, to a ruthless struggle for survival. He learns to shed his domesticated self and to seek backward, atavistically, through wilder and

Reprinted from Charles Frey, "Contradiction in *The Call of the Wild*," *Jack London Newsletter*, vol. 12, nos. 1–3, 1979. Reprinted by permission of the author.

wilder generations of forbears until he becomes, ultimately, the primordial wolf. The lesson, it would seem, for grownup and youth alike, is to slough off one's conventional self of civilization and liberate for action one's true savage being.

Such an account of *The Call of the Wild* as escapist fantasy (a fantasy with obvious links to the child-hero romances of Mark Twain, Robert Louis Stevenson, and Rudyard Kipling), though fair to the book in a sense, fails, nonetheless, to suggest its considerable complexity. For what Buck learns and becomes, as he struggles inward to the axis of his reality, amounts finally to contradiction. "The meaning of the stillness, and the cold, and dark," on the one hand, is "woe," and Buck learns "what a puppet thing life is," yet he learns, on the other hand, that "there is an ecstasy that marks the summit of life" and he becomes at moments "mastered by the sheer surging of life . . . the perfect joy of . . . everything that [is] not death."

CONTRADICTORY VIEWS OF LIFE

The contradiction in Buck (and, perhaps, in Jack London as well) between life as a woeful "puppet thing" and life as "ecstasy" may seem to diminish when we note that Buck feels the woe in his relatively few moments of wolf-singing, those lyrical withdrawals from unselfconscious action, whereas the "ecstasy comes when one is most alive, and it comes as a complete forgetfulness that one is alive." Ecstasy as forgetfulness, and anti-selfconsciousness theory, emerges as London's response to the pains of waking life, particularly life that cannot be enclosed by working or hunting. Buck finds that his fellow sled dogs, who are gloomy and morose, sour and sullen, when passive, become "utterly transformed by the harness." "The toil of the traces seemed the supreme expression of their being," and so Buck becomes "gripped tight by that nameless, incomprehensible pride of the trail and trace—that pride which holds dogs in the toil to the last gasp, which lures them to die joyfully in the harness, and breaks their hearts if they are cut out of the harness." Only in the Arctic snow and cold, by implication, moreover, are men and dogs forced to work so hard for sheer survival that all else can be forgotten. At night, Bucks drops instantly to sleep in "the sleep of the exhausted just."

Buck finds, however, that work in and of itself, even in the North, is not enough to guarantee the loss of pained self-

awareness. Not only does the work become excessive, me-
chanical, and finally meaningless, but the work that Buck
and the others are doing is part of a civilizing process in the
North, a process that attracts products of the Southland such
as Charles, Hal, and Mercedes. This "nice family party" that
has come from the States, as London is careful to note,
seems "manifestly out of place" in the rough Klondike region. Because they do "not know how to work themselves,"
at least in the unselfconscious way that has brought delight
to Buck, and because Mercedes remains "occupied with
weeping over herself," all chance of ecstatic "forgetfulness of
living" becomes obliterated. The dogs are forced to observe
and take part in a nightmare of bungling and cruelty. "By
this time," says London, "all the amenities and gentlenesses
of the Southland had fallen away from the three people." Yet
Mercedes, the one woman in the book, continues to seek the
comfort and chivalry of the South. Insisting upon them, she
nurses "a special grievance—the grievance of sex." Help-
lessness is "her most essential sex-prerogative," and so she
rides upon the sled, "a last lusty straw" to the burden of the
animals.

A Dichotomy of Values

London, at this point in the story, appears well on his way to es-
tablishing a wonderfully oversimplified dichotomy of values.
The sun-kissed South and its civilization become associated
with softness, effeminacy, dependency, self-consciousness, and
selfishness. The North and its frozen wilderness are associated with harsh struggle, masculine strength, independence,
and forgetfulness of self. One may add the dichotomy in London's allocation of spiritual values: Buck hails from Santa
Clara, his father was a Saint Bernard, his mother "a Scotch
shepherd," etc.; whereas the men of the North "cursing hor-
ribly" with "barbarous oaths" consistently call the dogs
"devils" and London describes dog eyes "diabolically gleaming," the pack's "hell's chorus," a rabbit a "wraith," the
North's "eerie," "ghostly" aspects, and Buck near the end as
truly "the Fiend incarnate." It would follow, then, that Buck,
seemingly launched on a journey from Southern values to
Northern ones, would drive steadily on toward an ever more
alienated and savage existence. London could have managed that by having Buck escape from the incompetent trio
from the States and then slowly recover his strength on his

own. But it is a tribute to this author's often-unrecognized complexity, his openness to contradiction, that Buck should be made to succumb first to the lure of John Thornton's "love" amid a fresh consideration of Southland values.

Buck comes to Thornton in the spring, when the "ghostly winter silence" has been momentarily banished by rising sap, young buds, newly active crickets, woodpeckers, squirrels, and "wild fowl driving up from the south in cunning wedges." The allures of warm sun, rest, play, feminine attention, and the like are all suddenly allowed back into the story. When a maternal Irish setter approaches, Buck finds himself "unable to resent her first advances," and she cleans him "as a mother cat washes her kittens." With the feminine element safely reduced to a motherly, ministering role, Buck is free to conceive a "love that was feverish and burning" for Thornton and his "rough embrace." This love seems, London admits, "to bespeak the soft, civilizing influence," but he will not let the matter rest there. Buck, he says, is no longer a "dog of the soft Southland," for he is in touch, irredeemably, with his primordial wolf self. He knows there is "no middle course. He must master or be mastered," and so Buck responds to the imperious call of the wild, the "blood longing" that defines him, ultimately, as "a killer, a thing that preyed, living on the things that lived, unaided, alone, by virtue of his own strength and prowess, surviving triumphantly in a hostile environment where only the strong survived."

Buck's Choice

Instead of being forced to adapt for survival in a hostile wilderness which he has been made to enter, Buck now leaves, of his own volition, the comfort and security of Thornton's hearth; his blood longing seeks out and creates for him the wild environment necessary for his self-expression. When he returns to Thornton's camp, he cannot stay long because a "restlessness" assails him and he is "haunted by recollections" of his wolf kin. London appears to argue that a rugged individualism is not only our best response to a harsh life thrust upon us against our will but is also the truest response to our inner alienated nature.

Yet again the contradictions appear. For Buck is not really a total loner: after Thornton's death, he becomes the leader of a wolf pack. If only, London seems to plead, those who

cannot submit to or who lose the possibility of civilized, domestic affection and comfort might find a society of their
own "half-friendly, half-savage" kind. Still the sense of contradiction surfaces in Buck as he returns each summer to
Thornton's deserted camp where "here he muses for a time,
howling once, long and mournfully, ere he departs." Even
there, however, London cannot leave the issue, but must go
on to insist finally that Buck "is not always alone." Throughout the long winters, Buck leads his fellow wolves, and sings
another song, "a song of the younger world, which is the
song of the pack."

Contradiction. Are we invited, at the last, to leave our fellows? or join them? To shun love? or seek it? To deny a middle way between dependence and independence? or to long
for one? To such questions, readers must frame their own diverse responses. *The Call of the Wild* provides no simple answers but raises a host of teasing possibilities. Therein lies,
surely, one secret of its wide and lasting appeal.

London's Work Is Full of Mixed Messages

Alfred Kazin

The Progressive period at the beginning of the twentieth century was fertile ground for political reform, writes eminent literary critic Alfred Kazin, but so many different influences were pressing for reform that the period was marked by energy, or "gusto," rather than coherent progress toward a particular social goal. London epitomized the confusion of mixed political philosophies. Kazin maintains: He called himself a socialist but worshiped violence like a fascist; suffused with fury in a hostile world, he remained a romanticist. Yet in *The Call of the Wild* he found what Kazin calls "the cold clear light of his life's purpose."

The significance of the Progressive period to literature is not that it marked a revolution in itself; it simply set in motion the forces that had been crying for release into the twentieth century. It was a catalyst, as Theodore Roosevelt, who seems in retrospect to have given the period so much of his own moral character, was one of its agents. The new spirit of insurgence had been bound to come, as the whole trend of American thought for twenty years and more had been heading in its direction. Yet when it did come, it became less a central movement of insurgence in itself than a medium through which flowed all the borrowed and conflicting European ideas, all the amorphous tendencies toward political reform, all the hopes for a different social order, all the questioning and nostalgia, aspiration and impatience, that had been dammed up so long at the back of the American mind.

The Progressive period of 1904–17 was marked by something more than "progressivism" itself, and it was anything but what a certain sentimental hero worship on the part of those who stood "at Armageddon" with the Progressive party in 1912 have made it out to be: a story of the conflict between liberal righteousness and evil that was written and largely directed by Theodore Roosevelt. By and large, as the social novelists of the period revealed, the Progressive period had no single "progressive" character, and many of its leading intellectual lights were not progressives in their own minds at all. What the period represented fundamentally was an upheaval, a sudden stirring, a breaking of the bonds between the old order and the new. Dominated by the spirit of reform, it was impatient with reform; seemingly revolutionary in mood, it had no revolutionary character. Stanchly middle-class in temperament, it helped to encourage the emergence of Socialism as a political power and saw the rise of proletarian revolutionary groups like the I.W.W. [International Workers of the World]. Yet its own Socialist novelists, like Jack London and Upton Sinclair, were the most boyish and romantic writers of the time. The Progressive period was, indeed, so much a repository for all the different influences that were now beginning to press on the American consciousness—Darwinism and imperialism, Socialism and naturalism—that those who think of it as a period devoted solely to muckraking and trust-busting and legislative reform must wonder at its delight in swashbuckling romance and "red-blooded" adventure.

OUR LAST BURST OF GUSTO

The gusto of American life had not yet died down with the spread of factories and the settlement of the last frontier; and it now welled up in one last tumultuous fling. Everyone had gusto in the period, or tried to catch Roosevelt's gusto. The Wobblies had it, the muckrakers lived on it, novelists like Frank Norris and Jack London and Upton Sinclair had it overwhelmingly. It was this that gave life to the new spirit of insurgence and carried it in all directions. The generation dominated by the dream of reform was a generation fascinated by imperialism; the period of Socialism's greatest growth in America was the same period that saw the worship of brute strength and talk of Anglo-Saxon supremacy. Roosevelt, who attacked the trusts and admired the Kaiser, railed against "malefactors of great wealth" and out of the self-consciousness of his own search for health preached "the strenuous life," set the tone. Just as Frank Norris, who

wrote the most powerful antitrust novel in *The Octopus*, worshiped bigness everywhere else, so even a leading Socialist
propagandist like Jack London found no difficulty in preach-
ing Marxian Socialism and Nietzsche's Superman at the
same time, and was indeed obsessed with the same imperialist worship of force and conquest that found expression in
Kipling and Houston Stewart Chamberlain's glorification of
the "great blond beast." That London seems to have thought
of the Superman as a Western work-giant like Paul Bunyan,
a brawny proletarian eligible for membership in the I.W.W.,
is another story; a whole generation of modern American
writers, from London to Mencken, now began to make its
own use of Nietzsche.

It was the shadow of power, of force, that lay over the
period, as Frank Norris had forecast in *McTeague* and *The
Octopus* and *Vandover and the Brute*, and as Dreiser was
now proving in his monumental portrait of Cowperwood in
novels like *The Titan* and *The Financier*. Roosevelt and Norris alike were fascinated by "vitality," and it might have been
Roosevelt himself, and not Norris, who said: "Vitality is the
thing after all. The United States in this year of grace 1902
does not want and need Scholars, but Men." Out of the self-
conscious exuberance of a young industrial republic that already was beginning to dominate the world scene, there
now emerged a grandiose pride, a thirst after bigness, that
was the counterpart of its own fear of bigness. There was a
fascination with energy in the Progressive period, with men
who did things, *big* men, that was reflected in Dreiser's and
Norris's tributes to the massive titans of the time, in Lincoln
Steffens's growing impatience with democracy and impending admiration of dictatorship, in the unconscious respect
with which the muckrakers described so carefully the immense power of the trusts. Darwinism had already presented Americans with the image of a power world in which
the strong were pitiless to the weak, and everything in the
world of contemporary industry and finance proved it. In so
short a space of years capitalism in America had become a
gigantic mechanism, a Behemoth that lay all over the landscape, absorbing everything for itself, brazen in its greed,
oblivious to the human society on which it fed. . . .

With the realization of the power of monopoly it was the
great middle class that now became alive to new dangers,
and with the failure of Populism the impulse toward re-

formism passed from the frontier to the big city, "the hope of democracy," as it was now called. Yet the general trend of Progressivism was not, as revolutionary workmen had hoped for thirty years, one of pure revulsion against the profit system; it was an attack on those who had lived too well on the profit system, on those who had destroyed free opportunity for others. Although often uncertain of what reform could mean, the Progressive spirit was channeled into reform, and it signified from the first a desire to bring the old balance of competition back; to turn, as the young Walter Lippmann said sardonically, even the workers into shopkeepers. For Progressivism had essentially one principle of action: it was nostalgic. . . .

The Progressive spirit was to mean many things before its time was up, but its historic significance is that it stirred up more than it knew. It worked toward economic and social legislation, for greater economic democracy, for women's rights, for more devotion and intelligence in public life; but indirectly it made men conscious of the changes needed everywhere.

The new spirit was abroad; there was change in the air. And everywhere one saw sudden stirrings in the literature that had been waiting for its charter of freedom. . . .

SOCIALIST NOVELISTS

In the eyes of the young Socialist intellectuals who were now beginning to come up, the muckrakers were bourgeois reformers who lacked a comprehensive grasp of the social problem; but they did not always claim that leading Socialist novelists like Jack London and Upton Sinclair were doing a better job. The Socialist intellectuals did not, in fact, seem to have too much respect for the novel, or for their own artistic achievements generally. It was a young Socialist critic named Van Wyck Brooks who commented at about this time on the social conscience in writers like Upton Sinclair which enables them "to do so much good that they often come to think of artistic truth itself as an enemy of progress." The scholars in the movement, such as Brooks and Walter Lippmann, were always a little appalled by the boisterous and raucous and inordinately prolific comrade-novelists like London and Sinclair. Socialists generally were proud that they had novelists of their own, but they must have wondered just how authentically their message was getting across. For the curious thing about these leading Socialist "fictioneers" is that they were the most romantic novelists of their time. London's greatest desire was to slip backwards, away from capitalism, into the lustier and easier world of the primitive frontier; Sinclair, as Robert Cantwell has pointed out, went back to the amiable faddism of a nineteenth-century visionary like Bronson Alcott, and was then, as he remains, the most enthusiastic and angelic of Utopians, a Brook Farmer who gave as much passion to vegetarianism as he did to Socialism and fiction. Indeed, both of these pioneer Socialist writers were amazingly like the romantic archetypes which benighted bourgeois opinion then made Socialist rebels out to be. To the America of Roosevelt and Taft, Socialism was still an exotic mushroom growth, though progressing rapidly—a movement too easily confused with surface phenomena like Sinclair's attempts to set up a Utopian community at Helicon Hall in New Jersey, or Maxim Gorki's expulsion from a New York hotel for living with a lady not his wife. Against this background, London and Sinclair, who lived and wrote in the feverish grand style of romantic revolt, seemed to suggest that Socialism was only a new and wilder romanticism.

Naïve the muckrakers were, but was there ever such a Dick Dare in modern American writing, so incarnate a confusion of all the innocence and lust for power in his day, as Jack London? Grandiloquent without being a fraud, he was the period's greatest crusader and the period's most unashamed hack. A visionary and an adventurer, like no other in his time he now seems cut off from the brave new world of Socialist comradeship to which he called all his life. In a period of "strong men" and worshipers of strong men, London the Socialist was the leading purveyor of primitive adventure tales. His Socialism was his greatest adventure, yet in nothing was he so tragic—and so impatient—as in his Socialism. A leading hero of the movement, he signed his letters with a dashing "yours for the revolution," but he was a prototype of the violence-worshiping Fascist intellectual if ever there was one in America; the most aggressive of contemporary insurgents, he was at bottom the most cynical. Yet like Norris he was pre-eminently a child of the Roosevelt-Kipling age, and his paradoxes were only its own. If he seems to be slipping away even as a boy's hero, he remains significant because his work, with its terror and bombast, is like a feverish concentration of all the adventurous insurgence and obsession with power that came to the fore in the Progressive period.

GRASPING STRAWS OF SALVATION

The clue to Jack London's work is certainly to be found in his own turbulent life, and not in his Socialism. He was a Socialist by instinct, but he was also a Nietzschean and a follower of Herbert Spencer by instinct. All his life he grasped whatever straw of salvation lay nearest at hand, and if he joined Karl Marx to the Superman with a boyish glee that has shocked American Marxists ever since, it is interesting to remember that he joined Herbert Spencer to Shelley, and astrology to philosophy, with as carefree a will. The greatest story he ever wrote was the story he lived: the story of the illegitimate son of a Western adventurer and itinerant astrologer, who grew up in Oakland, was an oyster pirate at fifteen, a sailor at seventeen, a tramp and a "workbeast," a trudger after Coxey's Army, a prospector in Alaska, and who quickly became rich by his stories, made and spent several fortunes, and by the circle of his own confused ambitions came round to the final despair in which he took his life. That story he tried to write in all his books—to depict himself in various phases as the struggling youth in *Martin Eden*, the lonely stormer of the heavens in *The Sea Wolf*, the triumphant natural man in *The Call of the Wild*, the avenging angel of his own class in *The Iron Heel*, and even the reprobate drunkard in *John Barleycorn*. He never succeeded fully, because he never mastered himself fully. That is easy to say, but London knew it better than anyone else. He clutched every doctrine, read and worked nineteen hours a day, followed many directions; in his heart he followed none.

If his Socialism remained longest, it was because its promise of a greater humanity made sense to him in terms of his bitter youth and the life he saw everywhere around him; yet Socialism, which also promised equality, humiliated his vanity. To Cloudesley Johns he once wrote: "Socialism is not an ideal system devised for the happiness of all men; it is devised for the happiness of certain kindred races. It is devised so as to give more strength to these certain kindred favored races so that they may survive and inherit the earth to the extinction of the lesser, weaker races." He never forgot the bitterness of his youth; the leading themes of all his work were to come out of it. Nor, since he could not forget his early sufferings, could he forgive society for permitting them. He determined, with the concentrated passion of the romantic ideal, to revenge himself, quite literally, upon that society. He would hold his place in it with any man, build the largest ranch in California, spend the most money, have the wildest time. He would assert his profound contempt for that society and its necessities by fleeing whenever he chose. His boat, "The Snark," to which he gave so many thousands and so valuable a part of his life, he conceived as grandly as any of his books; it was to be the medium in which he could assert himself as he had always failed fully to assert himself in his books. Instead, it became "London's Folly," and as characteristically mismanaged as his wealth and his loves.

It is the man of power, the aspirant Superman, who bestrides London's books, now as self-sacrificing as Prometheus, now as angry as Jove, but always a "blond beast" strangely bearing Jack London's own strength and Jack London's good looks. His Socialism was in truth an unconscious condescension; he rejoiced in the consciousness of a power which could be shared by the masses, a power that spilled over from the leader, as in *The Iron Heel*. His love for the class from which he sprang was deep enough, but it was a love founded on pity, the consciousness of common sufferings in the past; his own loyalty to it was capricious. What he said of his books he could have said with equal justice of his Socialism: "I have always stood for the exalting of the life that is in me over art, or any other extraneous thing." For one of his most powerful books, *The People of the Abyss*, he lived in London for months as a tramp, searching with the derelicts for food in the garbage thrown by prosperous householders into the mud. After reporting on the half-million and more of those "creatures dying miserably at the bottom of the social pit called London," he quoted with grim approval Theodore Parker's judgment of half a century before: "England is the paradise of the rich, the purgatory of the wise, and the hell of the poor." Yet for all his passionate sympathy with the sufferings of the poor, in England and America, his role as the "first working-class writer" carried no responsibility to the working class with it. He was a working-class writer because the fortunes of that class provided his only major experience; but he had no scruples about cheapening his work when the market for which he wrote compelled him to. Dreiser put it unforgettably when he wrote of London: "He did not feel that he cared for want and public indifference. Hence his many excellent romances."

A WORLD OF VIOLENCE

For if London is remembered as one of the first Socialist novelists of the modern age, he should also be remembered as one of the pioneers of the *Argosy* story tradition. By 1913 he could boast that he was the best-known and highest-paid writer in the world, and he had reached that eminence by cultivating the vein of Wild West romance. Yet in his many novels and stories of adventure he was not always writing as a deliberate hack. He never believed in any strength equal to his, for that strength had come from his own self-assertion; and out of his worship of strength and force came his delight in violence. He had proved himself by it, as seaman and adventurer, and it was by violence that his greatest characters came to live. For violence was their only avenue of expression in a world which, as London conceived it, was a testing-ground for the strong; violence expressed the truth of life, both the violence of the naturalist creed and the violence of superior men and women. Needless to say, it was London himself who spoke through Wolf Larsen, that Zolaesque Captain Ahab in *The Sea Wolf,* when he said: "I believe that life is a mess. It is like yeast, a ferment, a thing that moves or may move for a minute, an hour, a year, or a hundred years, but that in the end will cease to move. The big eat the little that they may continue to move, the strong eat the weak that they retain their strength. The lucky eat the most and move the longest, that is all." So all his primitive heroes, from Wolf Larsen to Martin Eden and Ernest Everhard, the blacksmith hero of *The Iron Heel,* came to express his desperate love of violence and its undercurrent of romanticism: the prizefighter in *The Game,* the prehistoric savages in *Before Adam,* the wild dog in *White Fang,* the gargantuan Daylight in *Burning Daylight,* and even the very titles of later books like *The Strength of the Strong* and *The Abysmal Brute.*

What his immediate contemporaries got out of London, it is now clear, was not his occasional Socialist message, but the same thrill in pursuit of "the strenuous life" that Theodore Roosevelt gave it. No one before him had discovered the literary possibilities of the Alaskan frontier, and he satisfied the taste of a generation still too close to its own frontier to lack appreciation of "red-blooded" romance, satisfied it as joyfully and commercially as he knew how. How much it must have meant, in a day when Nietzsche's Superman seemed to be wearing high boots and a rough frontiersman's jacket, to read the story of Buck in *The Call of the Wild*, that California dog-king roving in the Alaskan wilderness whom London had conceived as a type of the "dominant primordial beast"! How much it must have meant to polite readers, shivering with delight over "the real thing," to read a sentence like: "Buck got a frothing adversary by the throat, and was sprayed with blood when his teeth sank through the jugular"! Socialism or no Socialism, London appeared in his time as a man who could play all the roles of his generation with equal zest and indiscriminate energy—the insurgent reformer, the follower of Darwin and Herbert Spencer, the naturalist who worked amid romantic scenes, and especially the kind of self-made success, boastful and dominant and contemptuous of others, that at the same time appealed to contemporary taste and frightened it. For if it matters to us, it did not matter to London or his time that intensity is not enough. There was an apocalypse in all his stories of struggle and revolt—it is that final tearing of the bond of convention that London himself was to accomplish only by his suicide—that satisfied the taste for brutality; and nothing is so important about London as the fact that he came on the scene at a time when the shocked consciousness of a new epoch demanded the kind of heady violence that he was always so quick to provide.

A TRAGIC ROMANTICIST

Yet a romanticist he remained to the end, with all the raging fury of those who live in a hostile universe. The most popular writer of his generation, London was the loneliest; and for all his hopes of Socialism, personally the most tragic. Rejoicing in his adventure yarns, his own day could not see that the hulking supermen and superbeasts in his novels, while as "real" as thick slabs of bleeding meat, were essentially only a confession of despair. His heroes stormed the heights of their own minds, and shouted that they were storming the world. The early nineteen-hundreds read them as adventurers, symbols of their own muscularity; we know them all today—Wolf Larsen and Martin Eden, Burning Daylight and Darrell Standing, Ernest Everhard and Buck himself (London's greatest creation)—as characters in the romance London tried to live all his life. Like so many novelists in his generation, Socialist though he was, London wanted only "to get back," to escape into the dream of an earlier and happier society. The joke is that he reminded that generation—as he has still the power to remind us—only of the call men once heard in the wild, the thrill that could still run down a man's spine when there had been a wild, and life was a man-to-man fight, and good.

Was London the almost great writer some have felt in him, a powerful talent born out of his time? Or was he one of those sub-artists who out of the very richness of their personal experience only seem to suggest the presence of art in their work? It is hard to say, and perhaps, if the irony of his career is forgotten, he will be remembered as one of the last Western adventurers, a "pioneer Socialist" novelist, a name in the books, the friend of all those boys who want to run away from home. Yet it is good to remember that in at least one of his books that are still read today, *The Call of the Wild*, Jack London lives forever in the cold clear light of his life's purpose. For what is it but Jack London's own liberation from the pack of men in their competitive society that Buck, that Nietzschean hound, traces as he runs the pack out to forage alone in the wilderness? There, on the Alaskan heights, was London's greatest burst of splendor, his one affirmation of life that can still be believed.

CHRONOLOGY

1876

John Chaney is born January 12 to Flora Wellman, who names William Henry Chaney as his father; on September 7, Wellman marries John London, and the infant's name is changed to John Griffith London. Mark Twain publishes *The Adventures of Tom Sawyer.*

1878

The London family moves to Oakland, California.

1880

Thomas Edison produces and patents the first practical light bulb. The first major Alaskan gold strike occurs in Juneau. Lew Wallace publishes *Ben-Hur.*

1881

The London family moves to a farm in Alameda, California. President James A. Garfield is shot in Washington, D.C., on July 2; he dies on September 19.

1891

After finishing the eighth grade, London begins working in a cannery; after a few months, he purchases a boat and becomes an oyster pirate.

1892

Turning to the other side of the law, London joins the Fish Patrol to catch his former pirate colleagues.

1893

London joins the crew of of a seal-hunting boat that travels as far as Japan, Hawaii, and Siberia; this voyage provides the material for his first published story, "Typhoon off the Coast of Japan"; in August, he takes a job in a jute mill for ten cents an hour, ten hours a day. Hawaii is declared a U.S. protectorate.

1894

After briefly working as a power-plant coal heaver, in April London joins the group of unemployed men known as "Kelly's Army" in a march toward Washington to protest economic conditions, this was one of several "armies" following the example of Jacob S. Coxey, whose "army" of four hundred men reached Washington, D.C., on April 30; he leaves the group in May for exploratory "tramping" on his own and is jailed for vagrancy in New York for thirty days; he returns to the West Coast by train across Canada.

1895

London attends Oakland High School, publishing articles and stories in the school paper.

1896

London joins the Socialist Party; not finishing high school, he manages to pass the entrance test for the University of California and attends college for one semester.

1897

With his brother-in-law, he sails for Juneau, Alaska, and joins the Klondike Gold Rush.

1898

London returns to California, determined to make a living as a writer. United States annexes Hawaii as a territory. Victory in the Spanish-American War gains Guam, Puerto Rico, and the Philippine Islands for the United States.

1899

London publishes stories, essays, poems, even jokes; he begins a fruitful association with the *Overland Monthly*, which will regularly publish his works for several years. Theodore Veblen publishes *The Theory of the Leisure Class*, an outspoken assault on the rich.

1900

London marries Bessie Maddern on April 7; he publishes *The Son of the Wolf: Tales of the Far North.* The literary monthly *The Smart Set* begins publication; early contributors include London, Ambrose Bierce, Theodore Dreiser, and O. Henry. Wilbur and Orville Wright test their first full-scale glider at Kitty Hawk, North Carolina, flying it as a kite. The U.S. population has increased by 50 percent in twenty years and is now almost 76 million.

1901

London's daughter Joan is born on January 15; he runs for the office of mayor of Oakland but is defeated. Publishes *The God of His Fathers and Other Stories*. President William McKinley is assassinated.

1902

In England during the summer, London gathers material for *The People of the Abyss* while living among the slum dwellers in the East End of London; his daughter Becky is born October 20; he publishes *A Daughter of the Snows, Children of the Frost*, and *The Cruise of the Dazzler*. Congress authorizes the building of the Panama Canal.

1903

London falls in love with Charmian Kittredge and separates from Bessie; he publishes *The Call of the Wild, People of the Abyss*, and, with co-author Anna Strunsky, *The Kempton-Wace Letters;* Henry James publishes *The Ambassadors*.

1904

London serves as a war correspondent for the Hearst Syndicate, covering the war between Russia and Japan for the first six months of the year; Bessie files for divorce; London publishes *The Sea Wolf* and *The Faith of Men and Other Stories*. New York State passes its first speed limits: 10 mph in populated areas, 15 mph in villages, and 20 mph in open country.

1905

London tours giving lectures on socialism; he marries Charmian on November 19, the day after his divorce from Bessie becomes final; London begins purchasing land for what will become Beauty Ranch and publishes *The Game, Tales of the Fish Patrol*, and *War of the Classes*.

1906

London begins building the *Snark*, planning a seven-year, around-the-world cruise; he reports on the April San Francisco earthquake for *Collier's* magazine; he publishes *White Fang* (a complement to *The Call of the Wild*), *Moon-Face and Other Stories*, and a play, *Scorn of Women*.

1907

The *Snark* sails in April, reaching Tahiti by December; London publishes *Before Adam, Love of Life and Other Stories*, and the autobiographical *The Road*.

1908

After getting as far as Australia, London is hospitalized; the voyage of the *Snark* is abandoned in December; he publishes *The Iron Heel.*

1909

Jack and Charmian return to Oakland, touring Ecuador, New Orleans, and the Grand Canyon on the way home; he publishes *Martin Eden.*

1910

Jack and Charmian's daughter, born June 19, dies June 21; a seven-hundred-acre purchase expands Beauty Ranch to nearly one thousand acres; London buys the *Roamer* to sail in the San Joaquin River and San Francisco Bay areas; he publishes *Burning Daylight, Lost Face, Revolution and Other Essays,* and a play, *Theft.*

1911

London publishes *The Cruise of the Snark* and *South Sea Tales,* which make use of material from the ill-fated cruise of the *Snark,* as well as *Adventure* and *When God Laughs and Other Stories.*

1912

London signs a five-year contract with *Cosmopolitan* to write fiction for the magazine; he begins building Wolf House at Beauty Ranch, which now covers about fourteen hundred acres; he publishes *The House of Pride and Other Tales of Hawaii, A Son of the Sun,* and *Smoke Bellew.*

1913

Wolf House is burned to the ground; arson is suspected. London publishes *John Barleycorn, The Abysmal Brute, The Valley of the Moon,* and *The Night-Born;* he wins a lawsuit over film rights to *The Sea Wolf.*

1914

London spends two months covering the Mexican Revolution for *Collier's.* War breaks out in Europe. London publishes *The Mutiny of the Elsinore* and *The Strength of the Strong.*

1915

London publishes *The Scarlet Plague* and *The Star Rover.* The British steamship *Lusitania* is sunk by a German submarine. Pioneering birth control advocate Margaret Sanger is jailed in New York on obscenity charges.

1916

London publishes *The Little Lady of the Big House, The Turtles of Tasman,* and *The Acorn-Planter: A California Forest Play;* on the evening of November 21, he slips into a coma; he dies late in the day on November 22.

1917

The Human Drift, Jerry of the Islands, and *Michael, Brother of Jerry* are the first of several works published posthumously.

1918

The Red One is published.

1919

On the Makaloa Mat is published.

1920

Hearts of Three is published.

1922

Dutch Courage and Other Stories is published.

1963

The Assassination Bureau, Ltd. (completed by Robert L. Fish) is published.

1970

Jack London Reports: War Correspondence, Sports Articles, and Miscellaneous Writings (edited by King Hendricks and Irving Shepard) is published.

1971

Daughters of the Rich (a play, edited by James E. Sisson) is published.

1972

Gold (a play, edited by James E. Sisson) is published.

1979

Jack London on the Road: The Tramp Diary and Other Hobo Writings (edited by Richard W. Etulain) and *No Mentor but Myself: A Collection of Articles, Essays, Reviews, and Letters on Writing and Writers* (edited by Dale L. Walker) are published.

FOR FURTHER RESEARCH

Leonard D. Abbott, "Jack London's One Great Contribution to American Literature," *Current Opinion*, January 1916.

Robert Barltrop, *Jack London: The Man, the Writer, the Rebel*. London: Pluto Press, 1976.

Gorman Beauchamp, *Jack London*. San Bernardino, CA: Borgo Press, 1984.

Henry Meade Bland, "Jack London," *Overland Monthly*, May 1904.

Van Wyck Brooks, *Frank Norris and Jack London: The Confident Years, 1885–1915*. New York: Dutton, 1952.

Arthur Calder-Marshall, *Lone Wolf: The Story of Jack London*. New York: Duell, Sloan and Pearce, 1961.

Richard W. Etulain, ed., *Jack London on the Road: The Tramp Diary and Other Hobo Writings*. Logan: Utah State University Press, 1979.

Carolyn Johnston, *Jack London—An American Radical?* Westport, CT: Greenwood Press, 1984.

Alfred Kazin, *On Native Grounds: An Interpretation of Modern Prose Literature*. San Diego: Harcourt Brace, 1942, 1995.

Alex Kershaw, *Jack London: A Life*. New York: HarperCollins, 1997.

Russ Kingman, *A Pictorial Life of Jack London*. New York: Crown, 1979.

Charmian London, *The Book of Jack London*. 2 vols. New York: Century, 1921.

Joan London, *Jack London and His Daughters*. Berkeley, CA: Heyday Books, 1990.

James Lundquist, *Jack London: Adventures, Ideas, and Fiction*. New York: Ungar, 1987.

Scott L. Malcomsen, "The Inevitable White Man: Jack London's Endless Journey," *Village Voice Literary Supplement,* February 1994.

Stoddard Martin, *California Writers: Jack London, John Steinbeck, the Tough Guys.* New York: St. Martin's Press, 1983.

Joseph Noel, *Footloose in Arcadia: A Personal Record of Jack London, George Sterling, Ambrose Bierce.* New York: Carrick & Evans, 1940.

Susan M. Nuernberg, ed., *The Critical Response to Jack London.* Westwood, CT: Greenwood Press, 1995.

Ray Wilson Ownbey, *Jack London: Essays in Criticism.* Santa Barbara, CA: Peregrine Smith, 1978.

John Perry, *Jack London: An American Myth.* Chicago: Nelson-Hall, 1981.

Joan Sherman, *Jack London: A Reference Guide.* Boston: G.K. Hall, 1977.

Alfred S. Shivers, "The Romantic in Jack London: Far Away Frozen Wilderness," *Alaska Review,* vol. 1, no. 1, 1964.

Andrew Sinclair, *Jack: A Biography of Jack London.* New York: Harper & Row, 1977.

Clarice Stasz, *American Dreamers: Charmian and Jack London.* New York: St. Martin's Press, 1988.

Jacqueline Tavernier-Courbin, The Call of the Wild: *A Naturalistic Romance.* New York: Twayne, 1994.

———, ed., *Critical Essays on Jack London.* Boston: G.K. Hall, 1983.

Dale Walker, *The Alien Worlds of Jack London.* Grand Rapids, MI: Wolf House Books, 1973.

Franklin Walker, *Jack London and the Klondike: The Genesis of an American Writer.* San Marino, CA: Huntington Library, 1966.

Charles N. Watson Jr., *The Novels of Jack London: A Reappraisal.* Madison: University of Wisconsin Press, 1983.

Hensley C. Woodbridge, ed., *Jack London Newsletter.* Published from 1967 through 1988, this is the major source for London scholarship during those years. Available on microfilm.

World Wide Web

The University of California at Berkeley maintains a delightful collection of material on Jack London with links to a

few other sources of original material: http://sunsite.
berkeley.edu/London. The full text of *The Call of the Wild*
can be downloaded here, free; it can also be found on
several other sites. The Project Gutenberg site, http://
promo.net/pg/index.html, like the Berkeley site, offers
dozens of other works for download: http://promo.
net/pg/_authors/i-_london_jack_.html. Columbia University's Gopher will fetch the full-text versions of *The
Call of the Wild* and other London works; gopher://
gopher.cc.columbia.edu:71/11/miscellaneous/cubooks/
offbooks/london. Another site offering the full text of the
work is ftp://wiretap.spies.com/Library/Classic/callwild.
txt; since the book's copyright has expired, it is a popular
online text.

USEFUL EDITIONS OF *THE CALL OF THE WILD*

The following print editions of the book contain additional
helpful material.

Jack London, *The Call of the Wild.* With an Illustrated
Reader's Companion by Daniel Dyer. Norman: University
of Oklahoma Press, 1995.

Earl J. Wilcox, comp., The Call of the Wild *by Jack London: A
Casebook with Text, Background Sources, Reviews, Critical Essays, and Bibliography.* Chicago: Nelson-Hall, 1980.

INDEX